The Jazz Drummer's Workshop
Advanced Concepts For Musical Development

By John Riley

Modern Drummer Publisher/CEO **David Frangioni**

Managing Director/SVP **David Hakim**

Edited by **William F. Miller**

Design and layout **Michele M. Heusel**

Published by:
Modern Drummer Publications, Inc.
1279 W Palmetto Park Rd
PO Box 276064
Boca Raton, FL 33427

Subscribe to *Modern Drummer*, the world's best drumming magazine,
at: www.moderndrummer.com/subscribe

For fun and educational videos, subscribe to the
"Modern Drummer Official" YouTube channel.

Contents

Introduction

 Track 1

The Jazz Drummer's Workshop is a collection of columns written over the past ten years for *Modern Drummer* magazine. Each piece is an in-depth look at a specific drumming issue, almost like a private lesson on the given topic. In fact, many of the chapters grew out of issues particular students were having or from things I've worked on.

The book is organized into three sections—Concepts, The Masters Speak, and The Chop Shop—not in chronological order. Each chapter addresses, in varying degrees, the theoretical, technical, conceptual, and musical components relating to the given subject. Like life's lessons, some of these lessons will be absorbed immediately, while others will require considerable diligence. I play many of the examples on the accompanying CD so that you can hear the sound, balance, and flow of the material.

I see *The Jazz Drummer's Workshop* as a great supplement to my prior books, *The Art Of Bop Drumming* and *Beyond Bop Drumming*, as it covers many topics not addressed in them. *The Jazz Drummer's Workshop* fortifies the contents of those earlier books. I hope this material gives you insight into solving musical issues on the drumset. I also hope it leads you to a better understanding of the drummer's role in a band, to greater fluidity at the instrument, to a higher level of music making, and to more fun. Good luck.

Thanks

I want to thank the late Ron Spagnardi, *Modern Drummer's* founder and publisher, whose encouragement and support launched this project; Ron will be greatly missed. Thanks also to Bill Miller for his excellent editorial eye and constant enthusiasm; to Yamaha, Zildjian, and Remo for their great and innovative products and support of the music; to my parents and siblings for their nurturing and patience for all these years; and to my wife, Susan—thank you for everything. And finally, thank you to musicians *everywhere* for your continued inspiration.

Technical Info

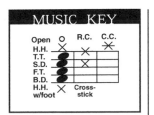

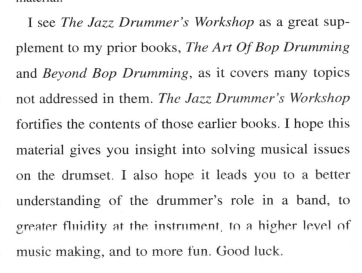

John's Kit (used on recording)
Drums: Yamaha Maple Custom Absolute
A. 4x14 snare drum
B. 8x12 mounted tom
C. 14x14 floor tom
D. 14x18 bass drum

Cymbals: Zildjian
1. 14" K Constantinople hi-hats
2. 18" K Pre-Aged Dry Light ride
3. 22" K Constantinople Medium-Thin High ride

Heads: Remo Ambassadors
Sticks: Zildjian John Riley model

CD recorded and mixed by Paul Wickliffe at Charleston Road Studio, Hampton, NJ. Mixed and mastered at Skyline Productions, Warren, NJ.

Chapter 1

Finding The Groove

You go into a club and the place is alive with energy. The band is smokin' and the audience is digging it. After one set you are both inspired and exhausted by the experience of hearing such a hot band. It's getting late so you head for home, but on the way you remember that another great band is playing just down the street, and you decide to pop in to check it out. Here the scene is quite different: The club is packed, but there is no "buzz" in the air. The band is playing, yet the audience is very passive: People are talking, and no one is bobbing their head or tapping their toes.

Some bands swing from the very first note. Others may not swing for an entire night. When a band is grooving, everyone feels loose and into the music; no one is tense. The players feel confident that they can play almost anything, and, at times, they are indeed "playing over their heads." How can a drummer create a good feeling every time he or she plays?

To answer this question, it might be helpful to step back for a moment and examine the ways that drummers and other musicians differ in how they appraise a good drummer. We most often speak about our idols in terms of how great their chops are or how wild their phrasing is or how wicked their bass drum foot is. But this is almost like "Drummers are from Mars, musicians are from Venus," because when another musician talks about his favorite drummer, his point of view is often totally different from ours.

Although music is a collective endeavor, bandleaders invariably talk about drummers in selfish terms—a great drummer is the one who plays in a way that allows the other musicians to feel that they are playing *their* best. Most bandleaders don't know a John Bonham lick from a five-stroke roll—and they don't need to! I've *never* heard a musician say that the reason that he hired a particular drummer was because of that drummer's chops. The bottom line is, people hire the drummers who make *them* sound good—period.

> If you seek to become a "name" band-leader's drummer, what you need to do is play in a way that makes that bandleader feel more comfortable and creative in his own playing than any *other* drummer makes him feel.

The intricacies of how a drummer creates that great feeling are immaterial to the other musicians. If you seek to become a "name" bandleader's drummer, what you need to do is play in a way that makes that bandleader feel more comfortable and creative in his own playing than any *other* drummer makes him feel. Once you've established that you can do that (which is obviously easier said than done), then you might get an opportunity to show the other aspects of your drumming prowess.

The way that we develop our skills shapes our concept. Most players go through very important formative periods in which they emulate their favorite players. They try

to play the ride cymbal patterns or the backbeats of their idols. They dissect and analyze. "If only I can phrase my cymbal beat exactly like so-and-so, then I'll be grooving!"

I went through the same process, and, at first, felt as though I *was* swinging just like my idol. But after a month or two of playing "his" time, I became unsure whether it was really swinging or not. At that point I became dissatisfied with my feel, and I searched for an even *more* swinging player to emulate in the hopes that adopting another master's approach would be the answer for me.

Through emulating a number of great players—the process consisted of studying and playing with their recordings and going to their concerts seeking direct musical insight—I gained many things: more control of the instrument; a familiarity with the different "dialects" of drumming; the realization that in order to become a great drummer one also had to be a great musician; an increased awareness of the importance of knowing tunes; some concept of what was expected of a professional musician; and respect for the mastery and the passion that

great musicians exhibit. What I *didn't* discover by copying people was how I could make a band swing. The reason for this is that as I attempted to play their time feel, I was more concerned with recreating their thing—"Is this the right way?"—than with creating a groove, and music, with the people I was actually playing with at that moment.

The things that my idols played worked well largely because they were played "in the moment." The ideas flowed in the context of that music, with those players, on that day. Their particular approach to playing the time grooved because of the chemistry of that combination of players. By emulating the masters, what I did discover was that, while each of my idols had a very personal way of playing the time, all the way from loose and on the bottom of the beat to tight and on top, there *were* certain similarities in their approach and feeling for music that I had to incorporate into my playing in order to swing.

Okay, so back to my original question: Where does the groove come from? Why does one band swing and another flounder? What is happening on the bandstand when the band is smoking? What is missing when a band isn't grooving?

As a tune is being counted off, each player makes his own appraisal of exactly what the tempo is. The song begins, and each player plays the tempo that they think was counted off. At this point the really good players are *all ears*. They are simultaneously playing their parts and making instantaneous assessments of how the collective groove is jelling. If there is a problem hooking up, the players will subtly adjust by moving towards each other time-wise and find the groove before anyone off the bandstand is even aware that there is a problem. There is never an "I'm right and you're wrong" attitude. Music works—whether it's Mozart, Miles, or Mötley Crüe—when the musicians are trying to play together. Players give up a little of their own individualism, their egos, for the sake of the whole.

The groove is communicated through the quarter-note pulse. A grooving pulse will definitely be metronomic, but the feel will be more "alive" when it is apparent that people, not machines, are providing this pulse for the enjoyment of others. The groove must feel uplifting, like it is moving forward, going somewhere without rushing.

As the quarter note is being established, the other players and the audience listen. After a couple of measures they start to anticipate exactly where the

comes into his head because it will sound great over this unwavering, infectious, unflappable quarter-note pulse.

> **Obviously music grooves most easily when the rhythm section is locked up. But playing in perfect unison isn't the only way to groove.**

quarter notes will fall. When the quarter notes are consistently placed exactly where the other players and the audience expect them, then everyone relaxes. The toes start to tap, the heads start to bob, and the musicians start to play with greater assuredness. Each player begins to feel that he can play almost any idea that

Obviously music grooves most easily when the rhythm section is locked up. But playing in perfect unison isn't the only way to groove. As long as the relationship between the bass player's placement of the beat and the drummer's placement is consistent, the music will groove. One or the other can be "on top" as long as the distance between the two is not *so* great that there is no center to the time, and as long as the relationship is stable. When one player tries to push or pull the other, it just won't groove.

Listen for yourself. Check out two swinging rhythm

sections: Philly Joe Jones and Paul Chambers with Miles Davis, and Elvin Jones and Jimmy Garrison with John Coltrane. With Miles, Philly Joe was always a little ahead of Chambers. Elvin and Garrison found that the opposite relationship was their ticket to grooving behind Coltrane. Sometimes a little tension between the bass and drums can add to the intensity of the music. The key to these two relationships was that the distance between them time-wise was small, and each individual played with a confident, consistent pulse.

Try this experiment: Record yourself playing to a CD. Set it up so that you record both your playing and the track, not just the drums alone. After you've recorded it, don't listen to it. Rather, record yourself playing to the same track again, but this time try to play on top of the beat. Don't listen to the tape yet. Record yourself one more time, this time playing behind the beat. Now listen to the three takes of the same song to see how much of a difference you can hear in the groove. Most drummers find that they have to adjust their interpretation of the pulse a lot more than is musically or emotionally comfortable in order to be able to hear any difference on the playback. The moral: We want to play together, so our "big adjustments" tend to be small in reality. Therefore most of the tiny discrepancies that we feel on the bandstand probably don't travel into the audience.

Your volume also affects the feeling of your pulse. If you play with a consistent volume, the time feels more stable than it would if you were frequently accenting randomly. The louder notes will seem to be early and the softer notes will seem to be late. So when establishing the groove it is helpful to play the quarter notes with consistent spacing *and* consistent volume.

Okay, we've covered some general thoughts about grooving. But what if you find yourself playing in an unstable rhythm section? How should you deal with it?

As drummers, when we are confronted with a bass player who rushes, drags—or has no center to his pulse and is just plain all over the place—we usually attempt to improve the situation by playing the time super-clearly. We'll attempt to "show" the bass player exactly where he ought to be putting the beat by nailing it even more precisely than usual, making our beat feel more pointed. But contrary to the intent, tightening up our time will invariably make the discrepancies between the bass player's pulse and our pulse even more obvious and troublesome. If a bass player can't find your time when you play in your normal fashion, forcing the issue by playing extra clearly usually won't help to make the music sound better.

A better idea is to find a way to play that "camouflages" the discrepancies in the time. To do that, I try to make my beat feel as *broad* as possible so that some "corner" of the roving bass player's beat will intersect with a "corner" of my steady beat and make the time appear to jell. Try this approach. I think you will find that making your time feel as broad as possible, rather than as pointed, will put the bass player more at ease, and that alone will help the music to groove.

To recap:
1. Open your ears to the other players. Play together.
2. Think like a musician. Make the other players sound good.
3. Play your own time—not your idol's.
4. Think consistent spacing and volume. Hypnotize with your groove.
5. When there are problems, play strong but become more supple, not more rigid.

Chapter 2

Holding The Groove

In Chapter 1, we discussed ways of finding the groove. Now we'll take the next step and work on *maintaining* the groove once you have established it.

Hooking up with the rest of the band, for an entire song or an entire tour, is critical in order for a band to groove and for a drummer to keep the gig. Once the rhythm section is "locked," the other players will play their best. Maintaining the "lock" is essential, but it can be just as elusive as generating one.

There are only two reasons why musicians lose the groove. First, they attempt to play things that they don't have control over. This leads to coordination problems and results in the groove fluctuating. Second, they lose their concentration, which also causes the groove to fluctuate.

To deal with these problems, I've found that practicing progressively more complex coordination exercises, while maintaining solid time and a clear, focused pattern on the ride cymbal, helps to reduce incidents of "groove busting." This type of practicing simultaneously addresses control and concentration issues. The concept is to gradually increase the density of what you can play comfortably and fluidly in order to strengthen both your reflexes and your mind. Playing complex stuff *in time* automatically improves your coordination while simultaneously requiring sustained, deep concentration.

Below are some coordination/concentration exercises to work on. These are three-beat motifs that are designed to challenge your control of your limbs and test your ability to keep your place in a four-measure phrase. The patterns start out fairly simply, but when orchestrated, become quite complex. These are just a small sampling of the types of things you could practice in order to create your own catalog of "puzzles" to master.

First, practice each three-beat motif while playing quarter notes on the ride cymbal. Once you are comfortable with that, go on to the four-measure phrases while playing the ride pattern. Work through this material slowly while counting out loud: "1234, 2234, 3234, 4234." The phrases must flow underneath your unvarying ride cymbal pattern. The numbered example in each group, i.e., 1, 2, and 3, is the basic pattern. Following each numbered exercise are orchestrations of the original motif designated 1A, 1B, and 1C.

After mastering a substantial amount of physically and mentally difficult material, you will gain a level of coordination and concentration that will allow you to play the most common grooves with greater ease and a deeper pocket. In other words, this added strength will give you the ability to "take care of business" while tapping a smaller portion of your resources. The end result will be that more of your brain power is available for you to check out and contribute to the bigger picture—the intensity of the groove, group dynamics, and group interplay.

An analogy: You buy a sports car that is capable of going 150 mph, but the maximum speed that you are allowed to drive is 65 mph. Car manufacturers describe the car's easy ability to exceed 65 mph as "headroom." The power available from 65 mph to 150 mph, which you will very rarely need to use, nonetheless translates to effortless functioning under normal conditions. Please keep in mind that additional drumming horsepower is useless, and perhaps even dangerous, in the hands of an unskilled (read: unmusical) driver—I mean drummer!

Three-Beat Motifs

Four-Measure Applications

Track 2

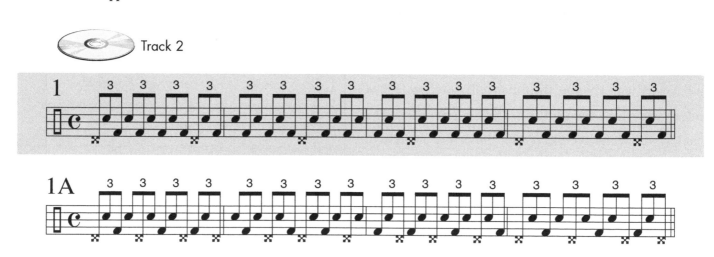

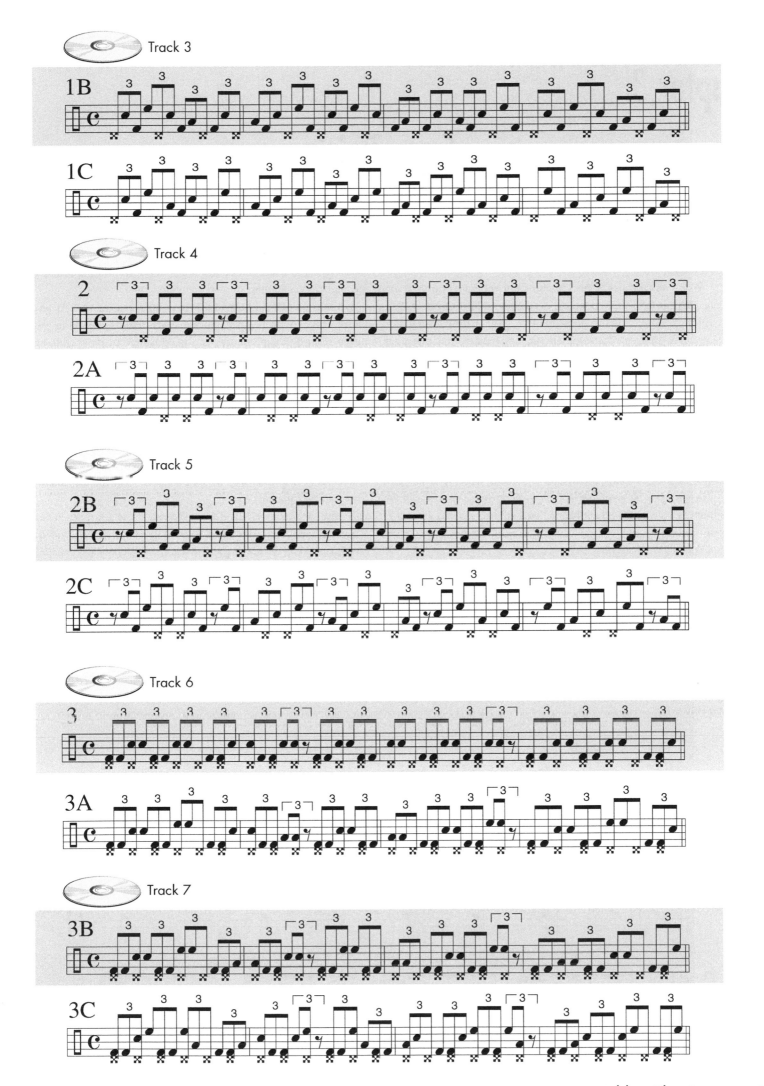

Chapter 3

Cross-Training

Cross-training is a performance enhancement philosophy that is used by sports coaches to improve the results of their athletes. The concept is that, in addition to sports-specific training—like swimmers swimming and runners running—skills will be improved by including periods of practice in non-specific but related areas.

While an ice-hockey puck weighs only about a pound, hockey players find that spending a considerable portion of their training time off the ice—in the gym lifting weights—improves their game. Football players have found that their performance on the field is improved by studying ballet or taking yoga classes. Professional basketball players are famous for their time spent on, and prowess at, the stationary bicycle and stair-climbing machine.

Drummers will find that by incorporating some cross-training into their practice routines they will increase their effectiveness on the musical playing field. I've noticed in my own practicing that upon returning to playing jazz after a period of working on non-jazz ideas, my jazz playing invariably feels improved. The source of the improvement is the strengthened "wiring" between my brain and my limbs through the practice and mastery of new non-jazz grooves or solo ideas.

I'm continually purchasing CDs and drum books, not because I hope to find the answer to some "secret" about playing, but to give myself the opportunity to regularly hear and play different things. Each month, when a new issue of *MD* arrives at my house, I read it cover to cover just because I'm curious. I play through each and every exercise because doing so makes me consider other possibilities and invariably sends my practice routine on some new journey. Several other cross-training approaches help make me a better player too. Reading through rudimental snare drum solos keeps my eyes and hands sharp. Playing the piano improves my feeling for melody and harmony. And exercising daily helps keep my mind and body strong, fresh, and alert.

While some people believe that they must master "American" music before they begin exploring other realms, checking out music from different cultures is a good source of cross-training ideas. Many drummers, myself included, have been intrigued by the idea of simulating the sound and feel of, among others, African, Brazilian, or Cuban percussion sections on the drumset.

There is a particularly interesting rhythmic elasticity or "rub" in Afro-Cuban music that is also found in other "world" musics, but that is foreign to jazz and rock. This rub is created by the simultaneous mixing of duplet- and triplet-based rhythms. Exploring this territory is a good way to improve your "wiring" and therefore your jazz playing.

Below are some Afro-Cuban-based cross-training ideas designed to help you develop a more authentic feel. These ideas were inspired by the playing and teaching of Frank Malabe, Louis Bauzo, Alex Acuña, Efrain Toro, Ignacio Berroa, Horacio Hernandez, and many others. Tito Puente's *Top Percussion*, recorded in 1957, and Michael Spiro's *Bata Ketu*, recorded in 1996, showcase burning percussion playing and exceptionally clear sound to listen to for clarification about the sound and feel of the music.

The following "building blocks" should be played at tempos ranging from quarter note = 60–120.

Building Block 1

Track 8

Groove Ideas

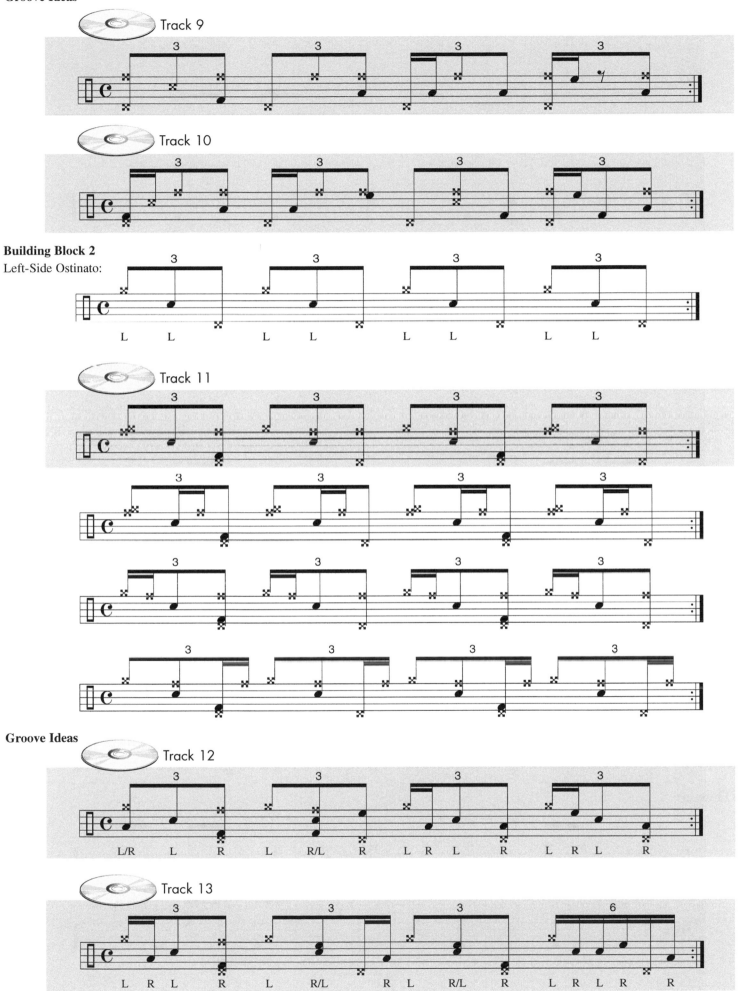

The next two building blocks feature faster "elastic" grooves. Play them at tempos ranging from half note = 80–140.

Building Block 3

Track 14

Groove Ideas

Track 15

Building Block 4

Groove Ideas

Chapter 4

Time Matters

While traveling around the world with different bands, I've seen many unusual billboards. With John Scofield in California I saw a Joe's Used Car Lot sign, which proclaimed that Joe was "The walkin' man's best friend." I don't know anything about Joe, but I do know that a sign seen outside a Holiday Inn in Kansas (while I was on the road with Woody Herman's band) is true. It read: "Improve your time and your time will improve you." Now *that* should be the title of a drum book!

Everyone agrees that grooving is important. But developing good time seems less of a concern—or possibly just more difficult—than becoming technically proficient, becoming a good reader, or learning to play different styles. However, having good chops, being a good reader, and knowing styles is practically useless if you can't execute your ideas in time. The drums are a foundation instrument, and the drummer's role is to provide the pulse that will support a given melody and harmony.

Here are four different approaches that will help you strengthen your time. They're probably unlike anything you've practiced before, so have patience and work slowly to attain the perfect balance and flow.

First, here's something inspired by blending Gary Chester's singing concept with Alan Dawson's approach to developing coordination. While playing the swing pattern with your ride cymbal and 2 and 4 with your hi-hat, play the written comping parts (in center box above) and sing the spaces. Use the syllables written—they're the ones that horn players sing—and be sure to swing what you sing. The result will be that between your snare drum, bass drum, and voice, all the 8th notes will be "played." This exercise will help you feel the spaces between the notes and make your phrases lay better. It will also help correct rushing problems. Start at quarter note = 70.

Second, while listening to a click set at quarter note = 90, play one of the one-measure phrases above (minus the singing) four times. Then immediately double your tempo so that the click is on beats 1 and 3 and half-note = 90, and play the same phrase eight times. Shift back and forth—sixteen clicks regular time, sixteen

Track 16

clicks double time—until you can make the change in tempo effortlessly. This will help in making transitions.

Third, experiment with putting the click on different beats in the measure. Everyone feels pretty comfortable with the click on the downbeats, but try grooving with the click on the swung upbeat, or on the "&" of 2 and the "&" of 4. Settle in, then try increasing your comping density and adding fills. It's harder than you might think.

Now set the click at 40 and think of that as the "1" of a groove at quarter note = 160. Try trading fours over that click. Double-time it and play at quarter note = 320. Here you get a downbeat every other measure. Try trading. With my old Dr. Beat I can set the beat counter on six, then tacit beats 2 through 6, leaving me a click only on beat 1 of what you can think of as a twelve-bar blues form at quarter note = 320! This is a real test of the steadiness of your pulse. You can even up the ante and trade choruses—play twelve bars of time, then twelve bars of solo, with only a click on the top of each chorus. This will test your stability and help your concentration.

Finally, I like working on my jazz feel by playing over hip-hop or pop tunes that have a shuffle feel. One of my favorites is Steely Dan's "Babylon Sisters" from the *Gaucho* CD. Take any of the comping ideas above, or some from my book *The Art Of Bop Drumming*, and repeat them many times over the track. Bernard Purdie's shuffle backbeat falls on the 3 of the swing groove. By repeating a simple phrase many times you'll find the best places to phrase your ideas. Use the backbeat on 3 as a landmark to measure your note placement. Refine that placement during each repeat of the phrase. Be sure to play all the "&s" of 2 as close to the backbeat as possible and all the "&s" of 3 as far from the backbeat as you can. Playing all the upbeats as late as you can will make the phrases really swing.

There are no quick or easy fixes when it comes to grooving, but consistent, conscientious work will make a world of difference. Improve your time and your time will improve the caliber of musicians you can work with.

Second-Line Applications

New Orleans "second-line" drumming is parade drumming done by a two-man drum "section." One man plays the snare drum while the other plays the bass drum and cymbal. These duos create hip, funky marches by building ideas in two-measure phrases. Their conversational syncopations are played in a fashion where they toss accents back and forth, rarely playing them in unison.

A typical second-line phrase is very balanced, containing the same number of accents on the snare drum as on the bass drum. If you've ever heard jazz drummers Billy Higgins, Ed Blackwell, Vernel Fournier, James Black, or Herlin Riley, then you've heard modern drumset applications of second-line ideas.

Here's a familiar second-line phrase written for snare drum, bass drum, and hi-hat. Play the snare drum part using alternating sticking. You can phrase this in single strokes as straight 8ths, swung 8ths, or as the Louisianians often do, "in the cracks" between straight and swung 8ths. You can also play the phrase as all buzz strokes (at the 8th-note rate). Listen for the counterpoint between the snare drum accents and the bass drum part.

Track 17

This accent scheme sounds really hip if you play the jazz beat on the ride cymbal and use the second line phrase as a comping idea.

Track 18

Here's the same phrase displaced by an 8th note. This one sounds great too—balanced, funky, hip, and swinging.

Track 19

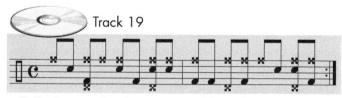

Following are the sixteen transpositions of this fundamental New Orleans phrase. Practice them street-beat style, jazz style with ride cymbal, with the shuffle on the cymbal, in straight 8ths with 8ths on a closed hi-hat or ride cymbal, and finally, with "in the cracks" spacing. These variations will generate grooves reminiscent of some of the things that Idris Muhammad, Bill Stewart, Jeff Watts, and Billy Martin have been doing lately.

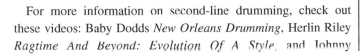

For more information on second-line drumming, check out these videos: Baby Dodds *New Orleans Drumming*, Herlin Riley *Ragtime And Beyond: Evolution Of A Style*, and Johnny Vidacovich *Street Beats: Modern Applications*. And also check out Chris Lacinak's book, *A Modern Approach To New Orleans "Second Line" Drumming*.

The Fast Face Lift

Playing uptempo swing with fluidity is a challenge, since your coordination and endurance are taken to their limit. Let's check out how an underutilized rudiment, the paradiddle-diddle—played RLRRLL—can spice up the comping flow and provide some relief from right-hand fatigue.

I first heard the paradiddle-diddle used at uptempos on the late 1950s playing of Elvin Jones. Today Adam Nussbaum and Jeff Watts use it to great advantage.

Examples 1–4 feature various foot combinations under the paradiddle-diddle.

Track 20

In example 5 the sixth note of the sticking, a left, is replaced by the bass drum.

Example 6 drops the hi-hat on 2 and 4 and adds an accent to each first left.

Track 21

Example 7 transforms the phrase into something thicker by moving the pattern between the ride cymbal and the drums.

Track 22

The final example incorporates the drums and foot combinations.

Practice these phrases at an easy tempo but work them up, because they sound best at tempos above half note = 130. Feel how each phrase crosses the 4/4 bar lines, and be sure to straighten out your 8th notes as the tempo gets above 140.

Chapter 7

3/4 Comping

Many drummers who feel very comfortable and sound very good playing and soloing in 4/4 find playing and soloing in 3/4 very restricting. Because beat 1 seems to exert an even stronger gravitational pull in 3/4 than in 4/4, playing too many 1s is a common tendency and stumbling block.

In this article we'll address comping in 3/4. The phrases below are designed to help you feel 1 without playing it; they will also give you some ideas for creating a looser and more fluid yet still solid feel.

First, play the ride pattern over and over again: ding-ding-ga-ding, ding-ding-ga-ding, etc.

Feel the 1 in the cymbal beat. Now select one of the three left-foot hi-hat patterns and play the "Two-Voice Comping In 8th Notes" phrases. Notice that the snare and bass parts avoid resolving on beat 1. Be careful to maintain the cymbal and hi-hat patterns. Practice the comping exercises with each of the hi-hat patterns.

Hi-Hat Variations

Two-Voice Comping In 8th Notes

Track 23 (with hi-hat #1)

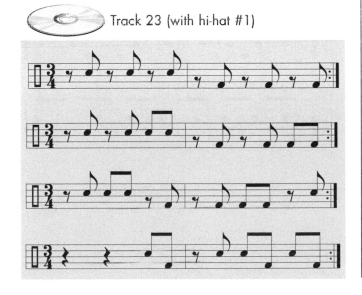

Two-Voice Comping In Triplets

Track 24 (with hi-hat #3)

Now, work on the "Three-Voice Comping In Triplets" ideas while playing the hi-hat as written.

Three-Voice Comping In Triplets

Track 25

3/4 Soloing

In Chapter 7, I discussed comping in 3/4. This time we'll look at how to develop solo ideas in 3/4. One way to create interesting phrases in three is to take a one-measure phrase in 4/4 and super-impose it over the 3/4 pulse—three measures of 4/4 is twelve beats, which equals four measures of 3/4.

Here are two different one-measure phrases in 4/4:

Check out how hip the same phrases sound when played in 3/4:

Track 26

Interesting 3/4 ideas can also be created by taking those same 4/4 phrases and manipulating any three of the four beats into one-measure phrases in 3/4. For example, the first phrase in the next group was created by playing the first 4/4 phrase material in this order: beat 1, then beat 2, then beat 3. In the next phrase the beats are in this order: 1,2,4. The third one is 1,3,4. Then 1,3,2; 1,4,2; 1,4,3. Then 2,3,4; 2,3,1; 2,4,1; 2,4,3; 2,1,3; 2,1,4; etc. Practice this material while playing the hi-hat on beats 2 and 3. Then go through it again, playing the hi-hat only on beat 2. Repeat each phrase until you are comfortable. Then, while playing in four-measure phrases, orchestrate each idea to include the toms.

Track 27

Roy Haynes

Finally, here are two eight-measure solos in 3/4 that Roy Haynes played on the song "Fly Me To The Moon" from his great recording *Out Of The Afternoon*. Listen to the recording and practice these phrases as written. Then "reorder" Roy's ideas, blend them with your own, or combine them with licks from above. Be sure to recognize just how flowing Roy's time and solo playing is throughout the CD, and keep in mind that Roy creates these swinging solos using very few ideas—placement is everything!

Chapter 9

Doubles Crossed

I'd like to give you some new ways to expand on the cross-sticking patterns on page 60 of my book, *Beyond Bop Drumming*. As originally written, these exercises are great for developing fluid movements and melodic phrases around the drums. For the best results, I recommend playing each measure very slowly at first. Be sure to remain relaxed—keep your shoulders down and your hands and forearms low. Gradually increase the tempo, but don't alter your relaxed "form." Here's the first measure from page 60.

Track 28

Below are some variations on these ideas that will show you other melodic and rhythmic possibilities. First, increase the density of the phrase by converting each stroke into a double stroke.

Track 29

The second measure from page 60 moves around the drums more than the first measure. Executing the first four notes might be a little tricky, but you don't really need crossovers to play them. Try playing the rights in the center of each tom and the lefts inside, towards the rim, so that the hands move parallel to each other rather than the right hand crossing over the left.

Here is the same phrase "doubled up."

These phrases also sound good when you incorporate displaced doubles.

Track 30

The example at the bottom of page 60 shows how these phrases can be played in 16th notes, creating phrases in 3/4.

The 3/4 phrases can also be doubled up.

Longer across-the-barline phrases can be created by combining these triplet and 16th-note cross-sticking ideas.

Experiment by adding doubles to this longer phrase. You should also apply these new treatments to the rest of the material on page 60.

When practicing, remember to remain physically relaxed. At the same time you must push in order to grow as a musician. The best results come from consistent, "conscious" practice. Build up new material by starting very slowly, thereby allowing your brain and muscles the time necessary to fully understand what you're asking of them.

Odd Times 1

In the 1950s and '60s, Max Roach and Joe Morello were the most visible and prolific explorers of rhythms in odd-time signatures. At that time, instrumentalists other than drummers were actively mining melodic and harmonic frontiers; very few musicians concerned themselves with writing odd-time music.

In the 1970s and '80s, Billy Cobham and Trilok Gurtu, both with John McLaughlin, reminded us of the potential in this untapped universe. Finally, in the 1990s, the odd-time pendulum had swung to the point where prominent composers and bandleaders actively incorporated tunes in odd times into their repertoire. Musicians Dave Holland, Steve Coleman, John Zorn, Kurt Rosenwinkle, Chris Potter, Branford Marsalis, and many others found odd times a great way to generate new musical dimensions and challenges.

Today everyone is playing in odd times. And just as drummers Max and Joe were the first to be comfortable playing odd times, bandleaders today look to their drummers to be quite fluent and solid regardless of the time signature.

One of the reasons odd-time music was less attractive to the beboppers was because the odd-time groove rarely flowed as smoothly or as effortlessly as 4/4. The rhythmic patterns of 5/4, 7/4, and the like always felt heavy and boxed in by an insistent "1" on the bass drum.

There's an old story about a famous musician who moved from New York to overseas. But after a couple of years he moved back to New York, and when asked why said, "Because nobody knew where '1' was over there!" Early jazz musicians often accented the first beat of every 4/4 measure, but by the swing era a smoother flow came into favor that has continually evolved. Obviously, that New Yorker wasn't looking for musicians who would play the "1" of every measure. Rather he sought those who could feel the "1" without having to accent it every bar.

A similar development has taken place in the modern treatment of playing odd-time songs, and that same ability is required; feel the "1," but don't *play* it all the time. In this series of columns we'll work towards that goal.

It's impossible to play in any odd time signature if you can't keep track of each beat in each measure. Before one can omit or avoid the "1," one must have a firm grip on *playing* the "1." We'll begin by working in 5/4, which is often subdivided into a three-beat phrase followed by a two-beat phrase—12345 is thought of as 12312.

Get comfortable with playing the following foot pattern, then add the ride cymbal pattern and play until it flows. (Also, be sure to swing all notated 8th notes.)

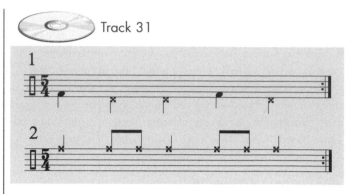

Track 31

Next we'll add melodic ideas to all the above, played on the snare drum. It will be helpful to count out loud.

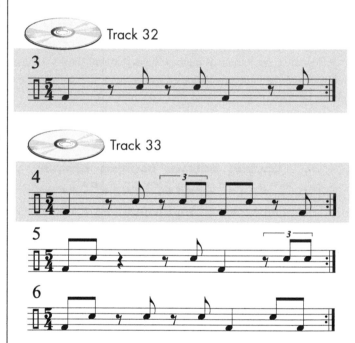

Track 32

Track 33

Now let's begin cracking open the "box" by varying the bass drum placement.

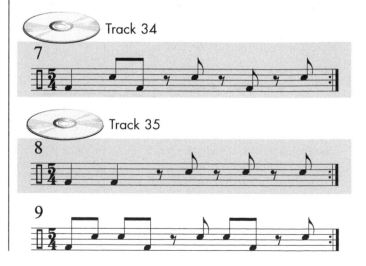

Track 34

Track 35

Practice each of the phrases with these ride cymbal patterns and hi-hat variations.

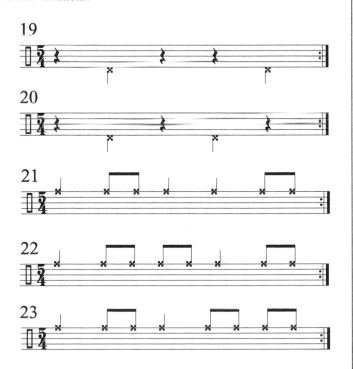

Your 5/4 grooves will start to sound hipper, less boxy, and more musical when played in longer phrases. While repeating each of the comps from above in a two-measure cycle, omit the bass drum or snare drum note that falls on the downbeat of every second measure.

Now, while stringing four of the one-bar comps together, omit notes on the downbeat of measures 2, 3, and 4. To help you keep your place, maintain a fixed pattern with your ride cymbal and hi-hat.

Once these phrases are flowing, experiment with loosening up your cymbal and hi-hat patterns. Allow the ride cymbal and hi-hat to "follow" the flow of the bass drum and snare drum syncopations. In essence, be less independent. While this approach will create the sensation that the time is more pliant, you must keep your place in each measure and play with metronomic solidity.

Odd Times 2

n Chapter 10, we went into the process of getting comfortable in 5/4. We then began to explore varying the phrasing. This time we'll get deeper into strengthening the ability to feel the "1" while simultaneously obscuring it.

1) Play the ride cymbal as if it was in 4/4, while keeping the other three limbs in 5/4. Practice this idea using phrases 3–18 and 24–31 in Part 1. And be sure to swing all 8th notes.

Track 37

2) Play the hi-hat as if it was in 4/4 while keeping the other three limbs in 5/4. (Again, practice this idea using phrases 3–18 and 24–31 in Part 1.) Then combine this hi-hat pattern with the previous ride pattern, and play the same snare and bass combinations.

Track 38

3) Last time we dealt with 5/4 organized as a three-beat phrase plus a two-beat phrase. Develop two-bar "mirror image" phrases (3223 and 2332).

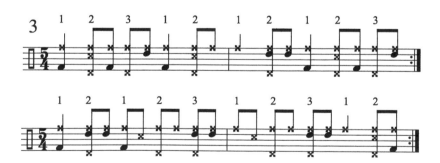

4) Divide each bar of 5/4 into two bars of 5/8.

5) Previously we worked on avoiding beat 1. Now we'll push the envelope further by accenting the points around beat 1.

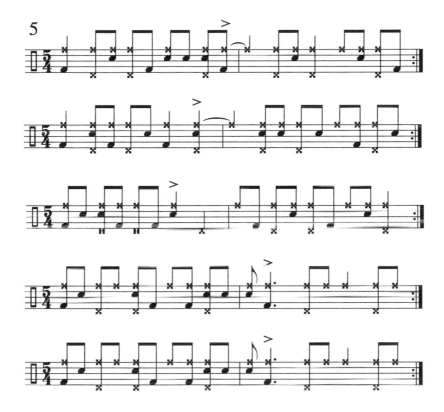

Finally, here are a few three-measure phrases, built on dotted quarter notes and based on an idea that Trilok Gurtu showed me. Once you get a grip on them, loosen up the foot ostinato.

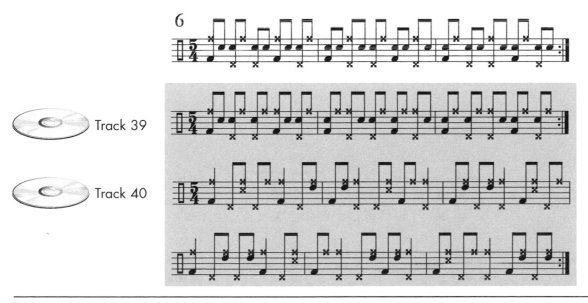

Track 39

Track 40

Your feeling for the time will continue to improve when you combine your favorite four-bar phrases from the previous chapter with the ideas discussed here. Practice this material with a metronome or drum machine set in a five-beat cycle. Once that's comfortable, play all the phrases while singing the riff from "Take Five" to yourself. I encourage you to apply all of these concepts to get comfortable in seven, nine, eleven, and so on.

Odd Times 3

The previous two chapters delved into ways to solidify jazz time playing in odd meters, focusing on 5/4. (Those same concepts can be easily applied to playing in seven, nine, eleven, and so on.) Now it's time to move into developing fluidity and solidity *soloing* in 5/4.

The best approach is to start with short solo phrases, and build from there. Play a four-measure cycle consisting of three bars of 5/4 jazz time, and conclude each four-bar phrase with one of the one-bar solo phrases shown in example 1. Work towards making the transition from playing time to soloing and back as seamless as possible.

These five-beat phrases are, for the most part, clearly constructed as a three-beat phrase plus a two-beat phrase. Maintain your hi-hat continuously on beats 2, 3, and 5 or beats 2 and 5 throughout your time playing and your soloing. This will enhance your flow.

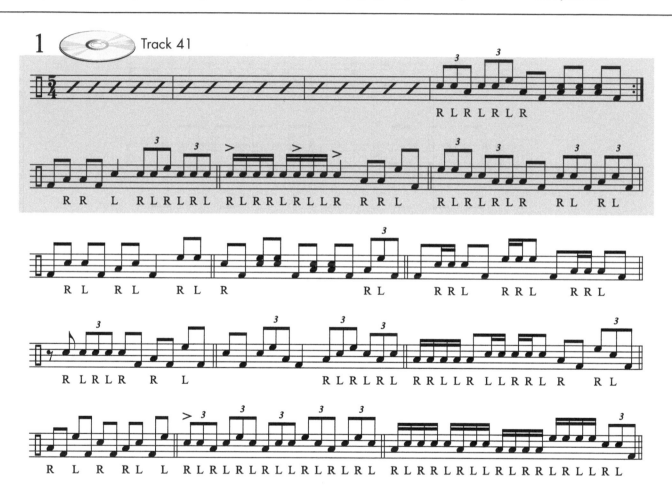

Now let's try two bars of time and two bars of soloing.

Finally, trade fours with yourself. Play four bars of 5/4 time followed by a four-measure solo. The solo can consist of combinations of repeated one-bar ideas or four individual ideas.

3

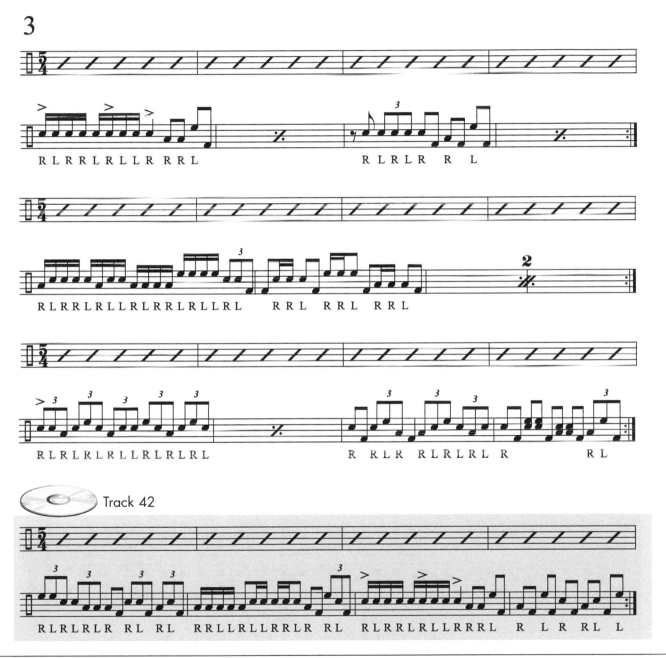

Track 42

Once these ideas are flowing, look for opportunities to play songs in 5/4. Try adapting a song that you normally play in 4/4 to 5/4. Play along with a 5/4 track like "Take Five," recorded by Joe Morello with The Dave Brubeck Quartet. The play-along CD *Turn It Up, Lay It Down Vol. I* includes a good tune in five to work out with.

In each case, start by grooving, then insert one-measure fills in the appropriate places, and then create a trading-fours scenario. Find a 5/4 vamp like "Take Five," and try creating longer flowing ideas—and steal some of Morello's beautiful phrases. Finally, work on soloing over a song form in 5/4. The previous examples are pretty dense; in a playing situation, incorporate dynamic contrast and the use of space to make your drumming as musical as possible.

Odd Times 4

Playing in odd times is fun and challenging. It gets even more interesting when common motivic ideas are played in 5/4. In my previous article, we worked with building solos by combining one-measure phrases in 5/4. Here we'll work in two-measure phrases, and we'll stretch the boundaries by employing 3/4, 4/4, and 5/8 phrases to camouflage beat 1 of the second bar.

Let's begin with ideas built from the six-stroke roll, paradiddles, and quarter-note triplets. Play two measures of 5/4 time before each phrase. Maintaining the standard pattern with your feet will be challenging at first, but doing so will help you keep your place. (Be sure to swing all of the notated 8th notes.)

Track 43

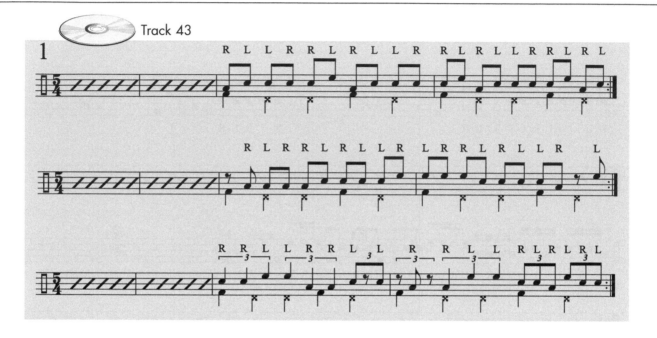

These phrases, based on two five-note sticking patterns, create interesting rhythmic counterpoint.

Finally, here are a few solo ideas based on common three-, four-, and five-note ideas.

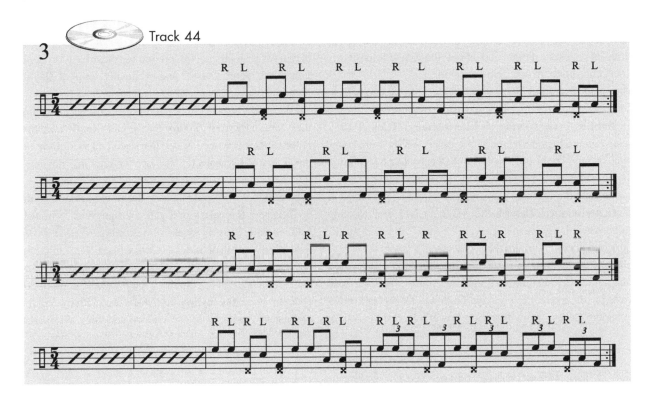

Track 44

I hope these four chapters on odd time playing have inspired you to explore the genre. Once you've internalized these ideas, try playing them without their respective foot ostinatos. Combine these ideas with those from the earlier column, and with your own phrases, to build longer solos in 5/4. Experiment with these concepts in other odd time signatures; the possibilities are endless.

Strive to eliminate musical boundaries. There should be no restrictions on your musical freedom and expression, regardless of time signature.

"Take Five" and more: Joe Morello

Chapter 14

To Transcribe Or Not To Transcribe?

As a young drummer, I had great fun playing with recordings. Sometimes I would use a recording as a backdrop, a kind of glorified metronome. At other times I would try to fit into the music I was hearing. This process taught me many lessons—about playing different tempos in time, about hearing the repetitions in a song's form, and about the limitations of my endurance, coordination, and concentration.

Playing with recordings also prompted me to listen carefully to songs and their drum parts. This led to attempting to copy the grooves and fills I was hearing on the recordings. I found that I could play some things perfectly, while others—even from songs that were easy to play in time with—were impossible to replicate. With the limited musical resources at my disposal, I could "fake" a groove similar to the beat that was giving me trouble, but I knew it wasn't exactly correct. Though I could read and was working through books with my teacher, playing "by ear" was, and still is, an important element in my learning process.

Eventually my level of musical sophistication and appreciation got to the point where I could no longer accept my "fake" versions of grooves I really liked. The breaking point was David Garibaldi's intro to "Squib Cakes," from Tower Of Power's *Back To Oakland*.

expression. The great thing about music is that you can pick who you learn from—you can pick your musical parents!

When I played my "fake" version of "Squib Cakes," I was organizing things that were comfortable for me to play. What I discovered after I transcribed it was that the things David was comfortable playing were really uncomfortable for me, like a foreign language. I shedded "Squib Cakes," and eventually some of David's dialect became *my* dialect.

I then went back to check out other recordings I had "faked" over the years. I transcribed Max Roach's playing on "Conversation." Afterwards, I practiced Max's language and more fully recognized the clarity of his dialect. Some of it entered my playing. By moving from approximations of another person's phrases (consisting only of things you could already do) to the actual material (which is often very foreign), you'll gain a deeper musical sensibility and become more actively involved in accelerating your growth.

I have *books* full of things I've transcribed. Some transcriptions are only two or three beats long, while others are entire songs. I still have the book, circa 1974, with the "Squib Cakes" transcription. It also contains some Harvey Mason, Mike Clark, Philly Joe Jones, Jack DeJohnette, and a lot of Steve Gadd and Tony Williams transcrip-

> "I play transcriptions to expand the kinds of ideas that I'm comfortable playing, not to copy things verbatim. It's a kind of physical and mental lubricant."

I *had* to figure it out. With pencil, paper, and erasers at hand, I listened to "Squib Cakes" over…and over…and over. Eventually I was able to accurately write out the intro. My realization of the value of transcribing, not to mention being able to see what David actually *played*, forever changed my approach to learning.

If you've seen my books or read my recent columns in *MD*, you'll know that I value transcriptions for this simple reason: The old cliché that music is a language is true. Music is best learned the same way we learn any other language. How do we learn to speak? First we copy the sounds our parents make. Eventually we come to understand the meanings of those sounds. Finally, we arrange those sounds to convey our point of view.

Music is the same. We copy things we hear. Eventually we realize why someone played what they played. Finally, we organize the things we've learned from others into our own personal form of

tions. Every couple of years I stumble upon that book and play through it again. I continue to discover hip ideas that I haven't fully explored and digested. I've also been intrigued by solos played by other instrumentalists, and have transcribed piano and horn solos and taken ideas from those to the kit.

A student of mine once balked at my suggestion that he transcribe a solo by Philly Joe Jones. He was concerned that he might select a solo that Philly Joe might not have liked. I told him that it wasn't important whether Philly Joe liked that particular solo, it was only important that *he* liked the solo! Furthermore, it's quite likely that if a student learned a solo that an artist played but didn't particularly care for, then the student would most likely be developing ideas that that artist hadn't fully explored.

At first, copying verbatim is exactly what everyone needs to do—just like you copy your parents' speech patterns to learn new words, new phrases, and the subtleties of the language. At this point, though, I play transcriptions to expand the kinds of ideas that I'm comfortable playing, not to copy things verbatim. It's a kind of physical and mental lubricant. But in the end I don't really speak like my parents do, and I don't sound like the people that I've transcribed. I just hope to be able to communicate fluently in both languages.

So how do you start? First of all, transcribing is tedious work, so pick a groove or solo that you really love. But select something that you think will be easy to notate. I promise it will take longer than you think to make it perfect.

Start by listening and counting through the groove several times to get a feel for the landmarks. Next decide on a time signature. Be sure to take into consideration which kind of notation you'll be most comfortable reading when you take the transcription to the kit. For example, do you prefer to read 8th notes in a fast tempo or 16th notes at half the speed? If I'm transcribing a groove, I'll often work from the top (ride cymbal or hi-hat) down, as the top part is often the most consistent. After I notate the top part, I'll fill in the more fluid stuff.

When transcribing a solo, I start by listening and counting through it. I do this to help me hear the phrases and to determine exactly how many measures long the solo is. As I listen, I make mental notes about how the phrases are shaped. Are they symmetrical, or do they go across the bar line? Where?

After hearing a solo a couple of times, I'll have a pretty good understanding of the basic shape. I start transcribing at the beginning of the solo, but if at some point I get stumped, I'll skip to the next phrase that I can hear clearly and continue from there. Often by the time I've written out the rest of the solo, I'll have a better understanding of that player's dialect. Then I can go back to the stuff that stumped me and figure it out with greater ease.

I prefer to transcribe from audio, not video. Watching a video offers too many distractions, making it difficult to focus on the specific measure at hand. So if I see some captivating playing on video, I'll transfer it to cassette, transcribe it, and then check it with the video later.

The reason to transcribe is to acquire information and knowledge. If something excited me enough to compel me to transcribe it, I want to do the tedious pencil work as quickly as possible so I can take the new musical ideas to the drumset as soon as possible. It's not cheating to slow the music down. For years I transcribed in real time. But once I got a tape recorder that had pitch control, I used it to help me hear the material more clearly, thus assisting me in writing it down quickly and accurately.

Last year I acquired an inexpensive digital machine that slows CDs or tapes down—an Akai Riff-O-Matic U400—and the sonic quality is much better than with cassettes. Digital technology is evolving quickly, so there may be even better options today.

The process of transcribing is beneficial on many levels. First, it improves your listening and concentration skills. Second, it provides new vocabulary. And third, transcribing improves your reading and writing skills. Plus, you can manipulate and permutate transcribed material, merging ideas from different sources more easily than things learned by ear. You can blend ideas from players from different eras: Take a page of David Garibaldi, mix it with some Max Roach, and then link that to some Jeff Watts. Give it a try. I guarantee it will open many doors for your drumming.

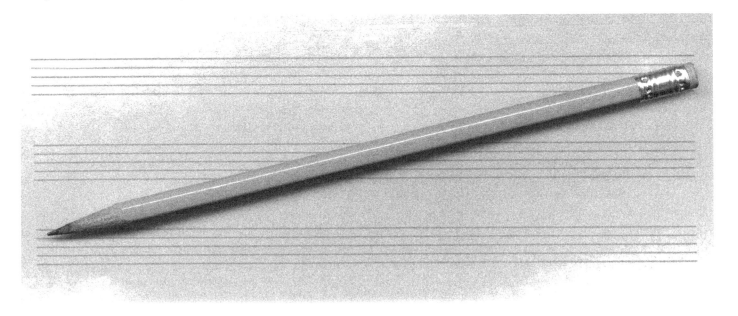

Chapter 15

Max Roach

Maximize Your Soloing

Several drummers, notably Kenny Clarke, Art Blakey, and Roy Haynes, have been honored with the title "Father Of Modern Drumming." But the title is most often—and perhaps most aptly—bestowed upon Mr. Max Roach.

Max grew up in Brooklyn, New York and as a youngster studied drums and piano. He arrived on the professional music scene in the mid-1940s, just after Kenny Clarke and Art Blakey and just before Roy Haynes. This was a time when jazz music was going through a transformation from being *the* popular dance music of the day to becoming a more concert-oriented, serious-listening music. As a very young man, Max, through his work with Charlie Parker, Dizzy Gillespie, and others, established himself as a major shaper of this new music called "bebop."

As a member of the earliest bop bands, Max was given extensive solo space. He was also called upon to find new ways to accompany virtuoso soloists at a variety of tempos, some breakneck fast. Max accomplished this by emphasizing the time on the ride cymbal, as his mentor Jo Jones had shown him, while feathering the bass drum and interjecting occasional musical punctuations with his snare drum.

At times Max created a more substantial dialog by mixing snare and bass drum accents underneath his relentless cymbal beat and 2 & 4 on his hi-hat. The bass drum accents became known as "bombs," and as this music was formalizing during World War II, drummers that played a lot of bass drum accents were said to be "dropping bombs."

After years as a sideman with the greatest musicians of the day, Max had grown into a leader himself. By the early 1950s he began leading a series of top-notch and innovative ensembles, which he continues to do to this day.

Max is a fantastic soloist and is often called "the most melodic drummer ever." But when questioned about his melodic inventiveness, Max has stated that he is more interested in musical structure and thinks more about the architecture and form of his phrases than melody. It's this aspect of Max's soloing that I'd like to explore in this article.

Let's look at the structure of Max's solo on the thirty-two-measure, AABA-form song "Delilah," from the 1954 recording *Clifford Brown And Max Roach*. The song is played at a medium tempo, and Max's solo is preceded by one chorus of trading "fours." Max's last "four" leads directly into his solo chorus. The solo is played with mallets, and Max keeps "four on the floor" going with his bass drum and 2 & 4 with his hi-hat throughout. Max plays a four-piece kit with two cymbals. This is the sound of small drums with cranked calf heads. Max plays the solo with his snares turned off. His small tom is tuned higher than his snare drum.

The solo opens with a classic bebop three-beat, 16th-note-triplet phrase, example A (on the following page). That phrase is repeated and concludes on beat 3 of measure two. On beat 3, Max plays 16th notes on the snare drum as a "connector" to measure three, where he plays the same three-beat phrase again. On beat 3 of measure four Max plays a triplet "connector" that foreshadows his next melodic idea. In measures five through eight, Max develops that triplet connector idea, example B, and plays another classic phrase consisting of triplets on the snare and melodic ideas on the toms, example C. Note how he starts simply and builds. Measure eight concludes with a flam on the snare drum, which foreshadows his next move—the quarter-note-triplet flams around the drums in measures nine through twelve, example D. Measures thirteen through sixteen explore 16th notes around the drums, mainly in groups of six, example E.

Thus far Max has played sixteen measures, which he has clearly structured into four distinct four-bar phrases, each employing a different subdivision. Bars one through four are based on a 16th-note-triplet idea; in bars five through eight, 8th-note triplets are explored; bars nine through thirteen feature quarter-note triplets; and in bars thirteen through sixteen Max develops 16th-note ideas. Much is revealed by simply looking at this solo transcription. The architecture almost looks like Max is trading fours with himself!

In measure seventeen, the beginning of the bridge of the song, Max plays another three-beat melodic phrase, this time in 16th notes, which he repeats, example F. The second half of the bridge, measures twenty-one through twenty-four, is made up of two two-measure phrases. The first one is yet another three-beat phrase that relates to the preceding phrase, example G, while the latter is similar to the triplet ideas played in measures five through eight, examples B and C.

Max doesn't toss off his ideas; he repeats and develops them with clarity and intent. The last eight measures of the solo are similar in structure to a recapitulation in classical music. Max paraphrases ideas that he introduced earlier in the solo to bring the solo full circle to a mature and pleasing conclusion. There isn't any "filler" material or ambiguity in this solo. Max means what he plays, and he executes his ideas flawlessly.

The tempo of this song is moderate and could afford one the opportunity to play more elaborately and/or more bombastically. However, Max is a mature *musician*, one who is more interested in developing a solo that builds on the moods of *this* song rather than using his solo space as a showcase for technical theatrics. It's interesting that there is no interplay between the hands and feet in the solo, nor are there cymbal crashes.

Here are Max's main motifs to practice individually before tackling the entire solo. Pay particular attention to the stickings I've included; Max is super-efficient, so there are no awkward cross-stickings in this solo. Each idea flows best using alternating sticking:

 Track 45

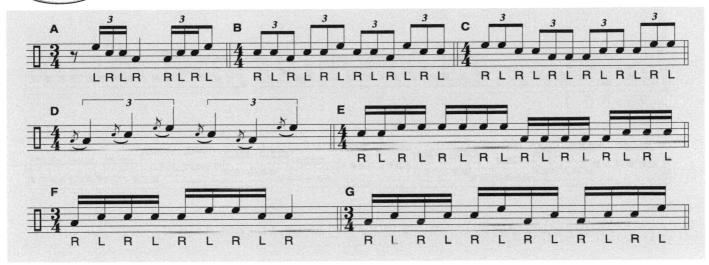

Now work on capturing Max's ideas, flow, and sound through the entire solo. Play it with mallets:

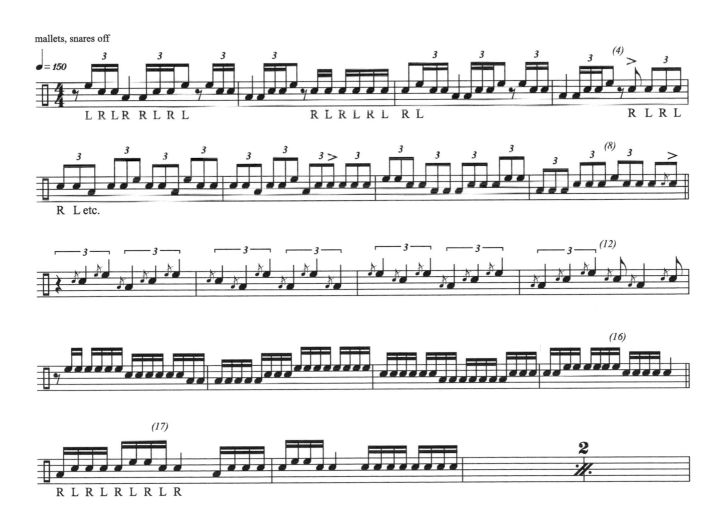

RLRLRL

RL R RL L LR   R

RL etc.

Finally, here are some more classic "Max-isms" as found in the five other great solos on this album.

Track 46

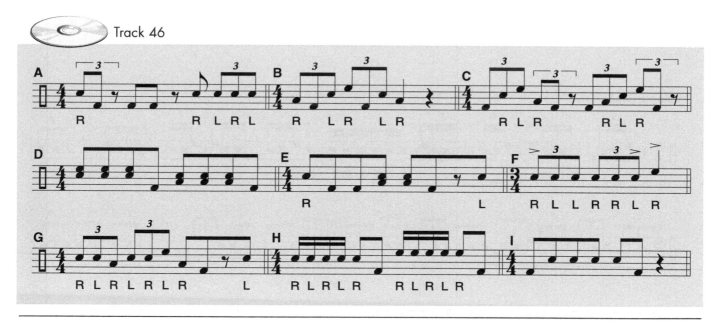

Study Max's playing on this album; it will really enlighten your playing. If you'd like to hear more of Max's great time playing, comping, and solo work, I recommend his album *Drums* *Unlimited*, as well as two others with Clifford Brown: *Clifford Brown And Max Roach At Basin Street* and *Brown And Roach Incorporated*.

Chapter 16

Billy Higgins Style & Analysis

Unless you're a hardcore jazz fan, you may think you've never heard the drumming of Billy Higgins. Never mind that he played on well over five hundred albums and three of the most popular—and sampled—jazz crossover hits of the 1960s—Herbie Hancock's "Watermelon Man," Lee Morgan's "The Sidewinder," and Eddie Harris's "Freedom Jazz Dance."

Mr. Higgins was one of the most sought-after accompanists in jazz. His buoyant, swinging feel was coupled with a great pair of ears; he always knew just what to play to bring out the best in his bandmates. Billy had a special warm and airy sound, and he played with great intensity but very softly. "I always wanted to hear what everybody else was playing," he explained.

Billy Higgins grew up in Los Angeles, where his first jazz influence was Kenny Clarke. Billy recalled to his childhood friend and fine drummer, Bill Goodwin, that he "based his whole concept on Kenny Clarke's playing on the song 'La Ronde,'" from a 1952 Modern Jazz Quartet/Milt Jackson Quintet recording (Prestige #7059).

Ceyton Call

In addition to being inspired by "Klook," Billy was also influenced by the other instrumentalists he was playing with and all the major instrumentalists of the day, like Art Tatum and Charlie Parker. As far as drum influences, Billy dug the melodiousness of Max Roach and Philly Joe Jones, Art Blakey's groove, Elvin Jones' comping, Ed Blackwell's groove orchestration, and Roy Haynes' individualist approach.

Billy first gained national exposure playing and recording with Ornette Coleman in 1958. Ornette's music was simultaneously swinging and free and required a new kind of suppleness and flexibility from a drummer. Through the years Billy shared the drumming duties in Ornette's band with Ed Blackwell. They were the perfect drummers for Ornette's open musical concept because they were able to hear where the music was going, support the new directions, and provide innovative accompaniment. To hear some early and freely innovative music check out Billy's "selfless" playing on Ornette's recording *The Shape Of Jazz To Come*.

In the 1960s, "Smilin' Billy," the appropriate nickname for this joyous man, played on hundreds of recordings with veterans like Thelonious Monk, Dexter Gordon, John Coltrane, and Sonny Rollins, and with the new wave of jazz stars—among them Herbie Hancock, Lee Morgan, Eddie Harris, and Hank Mobley.

Billy played the standard four-piece drumkit with two cymbals and hi-hat. He was a fantastic brush player and was also deft with mallets. In every setting, his mantra was the same: "The music is more important than the individual." One of my favorite recordings of his is Herbie Hancock's 1962 recording *Takin' Off*, and we'll start our inside look at Mr. Higgins' musicianship with this recording.

On "Takin' Off" you can hear that Billy got a beautiful sound from his instrument. Higgins tuned his kit fairly high, like most jazz drummers, and used a riveted cymbal as his main ride. The cymbal to his left was used more as a secondary ride than as a crash. Billy favored this type of tuning and cymbal sound during his entire career.

Conceptually, Billy was a "facilitator," not a dominator; he would enhance the direction that the music "wanted" to go in rather than impose his own will on the composition. You can hear that Billy was a master at creating a good feeling in the rhythm section. His supple ride-cymbal phrasing, which was based directly on Kenny Clarke's ride beat, has been admired and coveted by almost every jazz drummer to come after him.

Feathering the bass drum was also an important part of Billy's groove. Dynamically, he used the entire spectrum—but with great restraint. His snare drum comping ideas were often played as buzz strokes to lessen their sharpness. Along the same lines, he rarely marked the song form by playing a cymbal crash at the beginning of a chorus or at a change in soloists. His comping and overall flow was very precise but very legato.

On "Watermelon Man," Billy plays a straight-8th-note "booga-loo"-type groove, which became known by several names: "the Billy Higgins beat" and "that Blue Note funk groove." This groove is built off of the piano comp figure, but Billy finds numerous interesting ways to vary the pattern.

"Three Bags Full" is a waltz, and Billy plays some really hip and flowing across-the-barline phrases, somewhat reminiscent of Elvin Jones, to complement the melody. Notice how his comping propels the music during the solos; it's always uplifting.

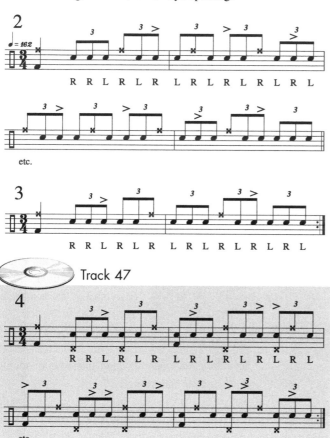

Track 47

"Empty Pockets" is a twelve-measure medium swinger. The head and first chorus of each solo are played with a relaxed broken feel, which evolves into a romping swinging groove. Here is Billy's treatment of the melody.

"The Maze" is another swinger, and during the head Billy plays off the piano comp. For the piano interludes, he goes to a nice broken "Latinish" Roy Haynes-type thing on the hi-hat. The comping is also characteristic, tasteful Billy.

"Driftin'" is an apt title for this cool thirty-two-measure tune. During the melody Billy plays a hip, swinging version of the "bongo beat" and comps superbly throughout. Here is the groove played during the melody.

The concluding track, "Alone And I," is a lovely ballad, which Billy supports with brushes.

Billy plays memorably on everything he recorded. Here are a couple more favorites. Lee Morgan's 1963 hit, *The Sidewinder*, features Billy playing a catchy "swing-a-nova" on the title track.

Another great recording is Dexter Gordon's 1962 classic *Go!* Billy plays magically throughout, but one groove in particular catches my ear—the brisk stick/brush bossa he played on "Love For Sale." (He played this holding a brush in his right hand and a stick in his left.)

Track 48

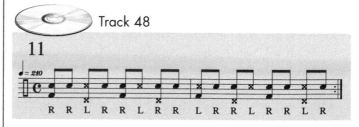

Another classic is Eddie Harris's "Freedom Jazz Dance" from the 1966 recording *The In Sound*. Here is the basic pattern, though Billy played endless danceable variations.

Track 49

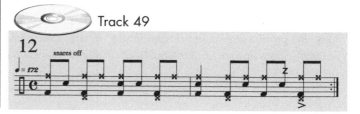

While Billy Higgins was a revered and renowned accompanist, he was also a great melodic drum soloist, and there are numerous "open" solos on his recordings with Ornette. While many drummers feel the urge to match the volume and "mass" of sound produced by the entire band when they solo, Billy always maintained his "cool" when he soloed.

One of my favorite Higgins solos is from *The Oracle*, a 1989 trio date led by pianist Hank Jones. Billy plays three choruses on the sixteen-measure swinger "Yesterdays." Notice that his solo definitely relates to the melody and that he uses orchestration to delineate the form and build the solo. The first chorus is built off of the ride cymbal, and the second chorus works its way onto the drums, developing triplet ideas reminiscent of "Three Bags Full." The third chorus is centered on the snare drum à la Kenny Clarke. Where appropriate, I've included the stickings that work best for me.

After hearing only one Billy Higgins recording, one would possibly come away from the experience feeling that he was "a good drummer." When you get into the body of his work, you realize that this man made a whole lot of *great* recordings. He always played with a mature, practical approach that was musically and sonically pleasing, and, most of all, his beat was always "inviting."

While playing, Billy was a joy to behold; he smiled continuously. His beaming attitude infected the other musicians, the music, and the audience. You hear the affect of his happy beat and joyous disposition on the recordings; everyone always sounded like they were having a ball playing together. As a testimonial to his understated greatness, many drummers would say, "But he didn't do anything." But most *musicians* considered Billy Higgins the perfect jazz drummer.

Billy, every time I hear you, I can't help but smile, and I know you're smiling too. Thanks for the great music and all the good vibes.

Chapter 17

Philly Joe Jones

Philly Joe "Fours"

Rudiments, even the well-worn paradiddle, are excellent building blocks for swinging fills and solos. On a number of occasions, I had the good fortune to watch master drummer Philly Joe Jones at very close range. Joe was a big fan of the rudiments and the Charles Wilcoxon books. I could see—and you can hear—that rudiments were a large component of his solo vocabulary.

Below are the four swinging "fours" that Joe played on the song "Four" from Miles Davis's classic 1956 Prestige recording *Workin'*. Each four-measure solo contains ideas incorporating paradiddles, but each is unique. Listen to the recording and learn these

solos. Notice all the variety and swing that Joe created employing only a couple of small ideas and playing them on a drumset consisting of only a snare drum, bass drum, floor tom, two cymbals, and hi-hat.

Mix and combine ideas from one "four" with those from the other "fours" to create new solos based on this vocabulary. Then blend these Philly Joe ideas with your own ideas to add some "roots" to your playing. With a foundation in these "fours," go ahead and learn the other fantastic Philly Joe Jones solos on this swinging Miles Davis CD. Have fun with these solos.

Track 50

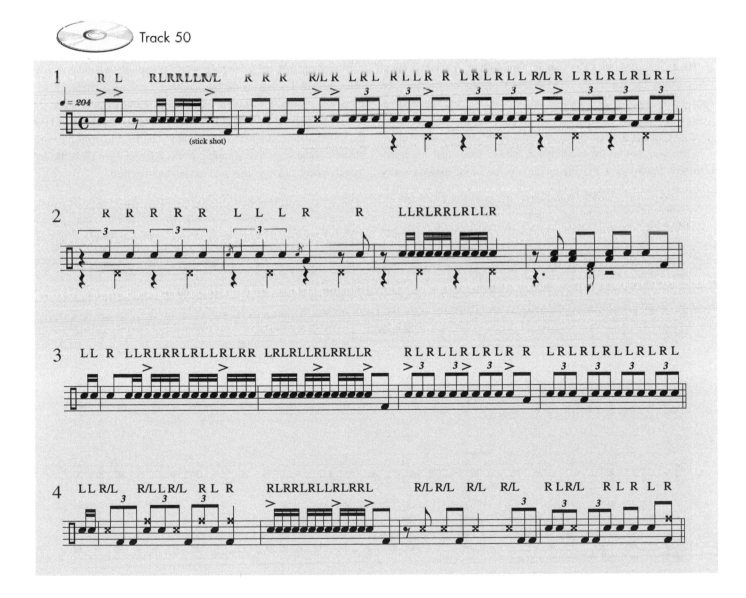

Chapter 18

Comping With Philly Joe

In Chapter 17 ("Philly Joe 'Fours'"), we looked at the great four-bar solos that Philly Joe Jones played on Miles Davis's *Workin'*. I hope you've listened to that CD and are in the process of digesting and experimenting with that vocabulary.

Philly Joe was undoubtedly a fantastic, creative, and slick soloist. But I imagine that his services were requested on so many record dates and with all those great bands primarily because his groove and comping were always super-swinging. In this article we'll examine Joe's playing on the melody of "Blues For Philly Joe," from Sonny Rollins' 1957 recording *Newk's Time*.

"Blues For Philly Joe" is a twelve-measure blues with a syncopated melody. Sonny plays the melody twice. Joe's playing displays that highly desirable but very elusive combination of great stability and intense forward momentum. On paper his playing isn't overly complex; he plays the regular cymbal pattern (except as noted in measures 18 and 24) and 2 and 4 on the hi-hat. Joe adds simple syncopations on the snare drum, and though he drops a few bombs with the bass drum, he feathers throughout. (The written bass drum notes are accented notes within the feathering.) The buoyant groove comes from the metronomic nature of his time and the hypnotic effect of his unchanging cymbal beat. Joe generates forward momentum by the exact placement and authoritative attitude of his snare drum and bass drum ideas.

When you look at the transcription, please notice that Joe rarely comps on beats 1 or 3. Playing on those points in the measure really diminishes forward momentum, so avoid them. Many less experienced players feel the need to accent the bass drum on beat 1 of every bar or so; when Joe accents with the bass drum, he likes to play it on beats 2 or 4.

Studying Joe's snare drum phrasing is also illuminating. First note the simplicity, then look for repeated ideas. The most common phrase is the one that runs from the "&" of 4 in the third measure through the fourth measure. That phrase is also played in bars 11, 16, and 23, and it has momentum because it "leads" to a 1 but doesn't conclude on it. By not resolving on 1, Joe's phrases keep moving forward, and they keep listeners engaged by making them hope for a resolution.

Interestingly, I don't hear a specific correlation between the syncopations in Sonny's rendition of the melody and Joe's accompaniment. I believe the methodology behind the construction of Joe's comping phrases lies more towards "goosing" the time along rather than playing off the melody. Joe knows that if the time feels good, and if the comping propels the time, then everyone will be happy.

It turns out that Joe's comping works beautifully with almost any blues melody. Try playing the transcription below while singing a different blues melody—"Straight No Chaser," "Billie's Bounce," etc.

Now try playing the first twelve measures of the transcription plus the last four measures while singing any song built in eight-measure phrases. Same story. The comping works because it isn't specifically melody-oriented, it's groove- and momentum-oriented.

Chapter 19

Elvin Jones Comping

Elvin! Few musicians create such a strong impression that we recognize them by their first name alone. But ever since the early 1960s, "Elvin" is all you've needed to say to conjure up images of intense sonic alchemy.

Mr. Jones was born (in 1927) and raised in Pontiac, Michigan and was the youngest son of a minister. Two of his older brothers, pianist Hank and cornetist Thad, made their own significant marks on the music world and helped young Elvin get started on the right track. Though Elvin was playing with fine musicians in the Detroit area in his late teens and twenties, he didn't make national waves until he joined John Coltrane's band in 1960 at the age of thirty-three.

Elvin had a very unusual sound and approach to playing the drums, of which he stated clearly, "I think of the drumset as one instrument, not a collection of instruments, and I take that single idea as the basis for my whole approach to the drums."

Early in his career, many musicians found Elvin's style confounding. They were not accustomed to having the time volleyed about the kit. Rather, they wanted to hear more consistent and repetitious rhythms on the ride cymbal, snare drum, bass drum, and hi-hat.

One musician observed that when he was playing with Elvin he felt like he was riding in a train that was going in one direction while sitting on top of another train going in the opposite direction!

Every time I've had the opportunity to play opposite a master like Buddy, Tony, Jack, Peter, Dennis, Vinnie, and so many more, I've been inspired to play the best music that I was capable of. That being said, one night at the Bottom Line, when I played with Randy Brecker opposite The Elvin Jones Jazz Machine, is especially notable in my mind. We opened the first set, with Elvin's band following, and they were on fire. After the intermission, we opened up again, but when I started to play, Elvin was playing *me*. I was not trying to sound like Elvin, but Elvin's spirit had taken over my interpretation of the music. His power, grace, ideas, and groove became the drumming accompanying Randy Brecker. I can't explain what happened or why it happened, but for that one set I was just inspired, subconsciously, in a way that I've never felt since.

Elvin, through the deployment of his "one instrument" concept, de-emphasized the traditional driving cymbal beat and hi-hat as markers of the pulse. This approach generated a rounder, more legato, yet still driving groove by spreading the time out around the entire kit. At one point the cymbal is the lead voice, at another it's the hi-hat, an instant later the bass drum and snare drum are prominent. Additionally, Elvin was the first drummer to comp while using vocabulary consistently stressing the middle note of the triplet. This creates the illusion of rhythmic elasticity, thereby generating the feeling of being on the "wrong train."

Here are some ideas to explore from the world of Mr. Jones. Traditional ride cymbal phrasing:

Elvin's ride cymbal phrasing:

While playing the hi-hat on 2 and 4 and keeping a consistent ride pattern, practice the following comping ideas (which stress the middle triplet note) as both one-measure and four-measure phrases. A good tempo to start at is quarter note = 60.

Track 52

Elvin varied his touch on the snare drum by doubling or buzzing the middle triplet note. Practice the following ideas as one-bar phrases, then combine them into a four-bar phrase.

Make sure that your snare drum phrasing is accurate; don't play the doubled middle triplet note as the "e-&" of straight 16th notes.

Here's the same idea in a three-beat cycle:

Elvin maximized his "one instrument" concept by completely integrating his hi-hat into the comping scheme. By playing the bass drum or hi-hat on the middle note of the triplet, he generated more variety, which resulted in an even more "topsy-turvy" feel. Play the hi-hat as written.

Elvin created long phrases by incorporating mixed three-beat motives, as in the following example. Be careful to keep your ride pattern steady.

Track 53

The ideas above represent "concentrated" excerpts of Elvin-like phrases. After you're comfortable with them and have worked through their intrinsic coordination obstacles, experiment with allowing your ride cymbal pattern to accommodate—i.e., follow—the flow of the other three limbs. This looser ride approach will help complete the "one instrument" vibe.

To have a better understanding of Elvin's intense approach, check out his video *Different Drummer*. Listen to the 1960s John Coltrane CDs such as *Coltrane Plays The Blues* and *Crescent,* or McCoy Tyner's *The Real McCoy*. The recent CDs by Joe Lovano (*Trio Fascination*) and Michael Brecker (*Time Is Of The Essence*) are also great and show that Elvin, at over seventy years old, was still playing with fire! My book, *Beyond Bop Drumming*, includes related information.

Elvin Jones was one of the all-time masters and truly one of a kind. Every serious player, regardless of style, can learn from and should have knowledge of Elvin's contributions to music.

Chapter 20

Elvin Jones Soloing

Imagine you're looking at an abstract painting by Picasso. At first you're unsure of what you're viewing, but shortly you begin to recognize eyes and a nose, and eventually things become a little clearer. The features in this portrait are in strange positions, and their proportions are very unusual. Though the portrait is abstract, it's clearly the work of a gifted and visionary artist.

To many a musician's ears, an Elvin Jones drum solo is even more abstract than a Picasso painting. A painting is in a frame, which creates an outline or border for the work. An Elvin drum solo is a fluid event during which the "frame" may not be apparent until the solo's completion. Furthermore, though Elvin rarely played a "free" solo, he was cunning in his displacement of musical landmarks, and his solo phrasing symmetry is difficult to comprehend—a solo's "face" might have three noses and…is that an eye? Some people have difficulty following the phrasing.

For me, Elvin's performances are very melodic and incorporate masterful facility, ingenuity, and passion. They're abstract masterpieces in their own right.

Elvin stated that he always played off of the melody, so the first step to "hearing" one of his solos is to listen to the solo while simultaneously singing the song's melody. This will help you hear his phrasing. You'll notice that the phrases can be several measures long and don't necessarily begin or resolve on beat 1.

Like his comping (discussed in the previous chapter), many phrases are made up of three-beat motifs, which go across the barline and, at times, across the phrase line. (The phrase line is a significant landmark in a song's harmony, usually every four or eight measures.) Elvin also liked to "shift the frame" by developing simple motifs—like right, left, foot—at various rates of speed.

Below are several three-beat Elvin motifs. First, practice them as individual-measure exercises.

 Track 54

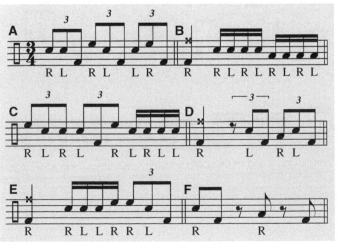

Now go back and combine the motifs into four-bar phrases to feel how they unfold across the barlines. To help you keep your place and internalize the phrases, it will be helpful for you to count out loud: "1234, 2234, 3234, 4234."

Here's a favorite time-stretching (i.e., "frame shifting") device incorporating a three-note motif:

 Track 55

Once you're comfortable with the previous example, experiment with reversing some of the hand combinations from right-left to left-right. Then experiment with substituting the hi-hat for some of the bass drum notes.

The triplet-on-triplet rate in the second half of measure three above contributes a lot of elasticity and mystery to Elvin's playing. He often shifted between the 16th-note rate, the 8-over-2 rate, and the 9-over-2 rate of triplets-on-triplets. Triplets-on-triplets can be best felt by practicing this exercise:

 Track 56

In the 1960s Elvin played the standard four-piece drumkit. In later years he played a kit with four toms, with his two floor toms often tuned lower than his bass drum. This tuning really opened up the possibilities for creating ear-stretching phrases out of the ideas above.

Finally, here's one of my favorite Elvin Jones solos. It's a very concise, passionate statement from Wayne Shorter's album *Night Dreamer,* recorded in 1964. "Black Nile" is a thirty-two-measure song on which Elvin takes a one-chorus solo. Check out the variety of material he chooses to develop, his long opening phrase with its

deceptive conclusion on beat 4 of bar eight, the three-beat phrases in the bridge (bars 17–24), and the solo's explosive final phrase.

Get the CD, sing the song's melody along with the drum solo, and learn this solo! I've included the stickings that help me approximate Elvin's sound and flow, but feel free to experiment.

Tony Williams Style & Analysis

The first time I heard Tony Williams was in Barney Lane's dorm room at North Texas. It was the first week of my freshman year, and Barney was my source; he was a transfer student, had been doing jazz gigs, and knew a thousand LPs.

Every night after the practice rooms were closed, Barney would play selected cuts of his favorite drummers. He would tell me, a jazz novice, exactly what was happening in the music, why it was happening, and why it was hip. Barney was turning me on to all of his special finds—Grady Tate, Mel Lewis, Eric Gravatt—guys who were really playing but weren't household names. Then he realized just how green I was: "You mean you haven't heard Tony?" he said with disbelief. The next thing I knew he was play-

ing "Seven Steps To Heaven," "Walkin," and "Joshua," all from the live Miles Davis recording *Four & More*, and my life was changed for ever. The following day I went to the record store and bought every record they had with Tony and Miles.

In the twenty or so years since that night, I've heard a lot of music and played some myself. I continue to enjoy and study the work of all my favorite players. But after all these years of living with Tony's playing, I must admit that I'm not much closer to unraveling the mystery of how he arrived at such an original concept, so fully formed, at such a young age. But I do know that whenever I feel at a loss for what to practice, all I have to do is listen to some Tony. Suddenly I become very inspired.

Early Approaches

Here is an interesting quote from Tony Williams that appeared in a *Modern Drummer* interview in 1984: "When I was a kid, for about two years I played like Max Roach. Max is my favorite drummer. I don't know if I've ever said this clearly and plainly, but Max Roach was my biggest drum idol. Art Blakey was my first idol, but Max was the biggest. So I would buy every record I could find with Max on it, and then I would play exactly like him—exactly what was on the record, solos and everything. I also did that with drummers like Art Blakey, Philly Joe Jones, Jimmy Cobb, Roy Haynes, and all of the drummers I admired. I would even tune my drums just like they were on the record."

One can hear very faint similarities to the players Tony mentioned as his main sources (though you certainly don't hear anyone else's licks). At slow tempos his ride cymbal beat is phrased kind of tightly and on top of the beat, like Jimmy Cobb's.

His occasional use of unison snare and ride cymbal figures is reminiscent of Roy Haynes' approach.

His irregular use of the hi-hat reminds me of ideas from both Art Blakey and Roy Haynes.

His up-tempo ride cymbal phrasing is very "flat," and he plays a lot of five-note ideas, similar to what you hear from Shelly Manne's playing years earlier.

The "snap" and virtuosity of Tony's solos communicates the same kind of feeling of command of the instrument that I hear from Max Roach and Philly Joe Jones. However, these comparisons are a very small part of the picture to me, not even as apparent as the shadow of a ghost. I seem to remember Tony saying in an old *Down Beat* interview that he had learned to play like his idols, and then created his own voice by playing all the things that his idols weren't playing.

My main impression of Tony is that of a master who invented his own super-sophisticated language for the drumset by blending bebop ideas with more abstract concepts of playing, ideas that he had heard in the avant-garde scene, while at the same time infusing the music with the energy of rock. This amalgam was not just a new way to play the drums, but a completely new way to play music. It appears that Tony made it his responsibility to take the music in a new direction by playing it exactly the way he wanted to play it. Fortunately Tony found in Miles Davis a leader with the temperament and the vision to encourage these explorations. But every band that Tony worked in sounded special due to his "go for it" attitude—he loved to take chances. And through his playing he compelled his bandmates to really stretch.

"Nefertiti"

On the following page is a transcription of Tony's playing of the song "Nefertiti" from the Miles Davis recording of the same name. "Nefertiti" is a sixteen-measure form, and this is the second version the band recorded on that day in June of 1967.

If you listen, you will notice that this performance is somewhat unusual in that there are no solos during the entire 7:49 take. I understand that the first take of this tune, done just prior to this one, was among the most amazing things that the band ever played, but due to some technical problems in the studio the tape was unusable. Upon learning that the first take was lost and that they would have to play another, the musicians were quite disappointed, and no one felt like soloing on this second take. However, what you do hear on the second take is prime Tony Williams; he completely directs the shape of this amazing performance by leading this slowly evolving, trance-like tune through a series of intense climaxes.

The accompanying transcription begins near the top of their ascent, at 5:20 into the piece, which is the beginning of the tenth chorus, and it continues for three choruses. Looking at this transcription will definitely give you some new drumming ideas. The "licks" are there for you to sift through, but I think your degree of

understanding and appreciation for Tony's level of musicianship will be infinitely more enhanced if you get this recording and listen to the entire tune—and the entire CD.

While there isn't space here to analyze each and every aspect of Tony's amazing thirty-plus-year recording career, in regards to this transcription, I'd like to point out some of his main conceptual innovations and stylistic tendencies. This sixteen-bar song is structured as two eight-bar phrases, and drummers traditionally would subtly delineate eight-bar sections by playing some sort of fill at the end of the eighth and sixteenth bars to show these musical landmarks. A big reason Tony's playing always sounded so fresh was that he almost never spelled out the phrases in such a symmetrical fashion. He intentionally avoided playing a big "1" at the top of a phrase, preferring instead to create deceptive cadences. He did this in several different ways:

A) by playing a fill that sounded like it was going to end on the "1" but continuing past the normal resolution point to a later accent

B) by playing a fill that climaxed early—very often on one of the two most unsettling points in the measure—the & of beats 1 or 3 before a big 1

C) by ending his fill, either before or after beat 1, and returning to the ride cymbal without playing any accent at all, giving us the "build up" but not the resolution "crash."

You can see examples of these techniques in bars 4, 8, 9, 16, 20, and continually throughout the chart. All of these devices kept the music from "resting" too much; they pushed it forward in search of a real resolution.

Other innovations include Tony's use of "odd" groups of notes, like the five-note motif he explores in measures 13 and 14, and his use of metric modulation, or the variable-speed phrase, as in the shift from bar 21 to 22. Measures 25-27 are an emotional peak in the performance. Notice how Tony's energy changes the music, and then how he releases that energy in bars 28-32.

Measure 33 is the beginning of the third transcribed chorus (6:30 on the CD). At this point Miles and Wayne Shorter stopped playing the melody. Observe how patient Tony was, as well as the dramatic effect of his diminuendo and crescendo in measures 33-36. This chorus became a drum interlude before the melody returned, and Tony shaped it beautifully.

To end the song, the band played the melody one final time. Tony wound the intensity up briefly, then went way down, ending the tune by playing very softly and simply—just as the song began.

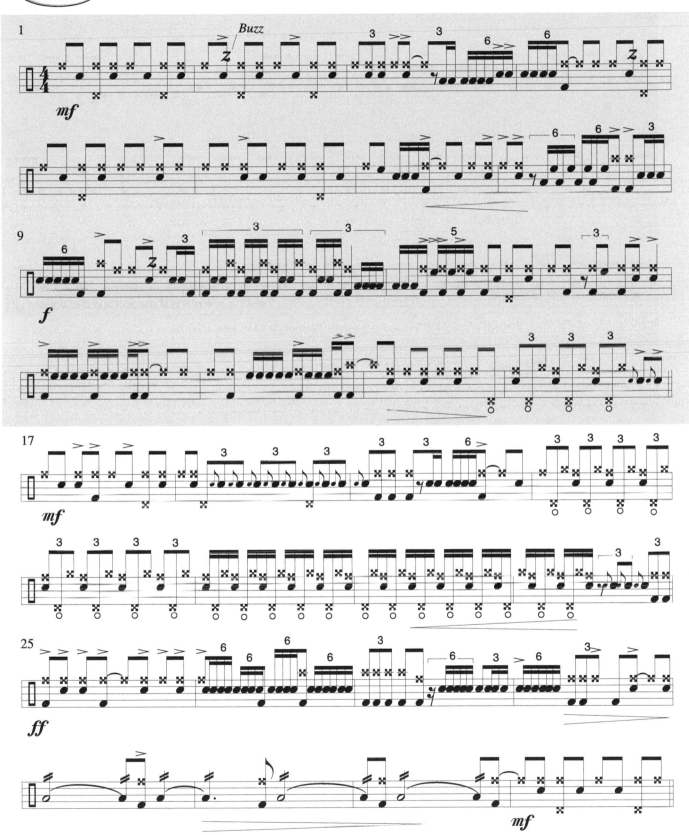

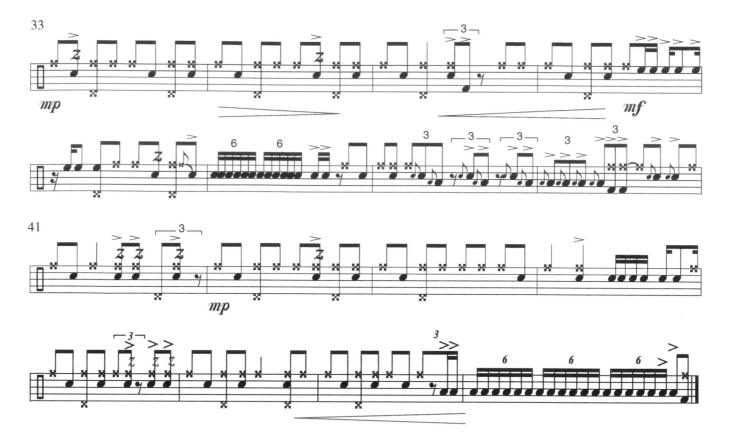

The Sound

Tony's unique sound and touch were important factors in his music-making. His sound was very clean, which is directly from the bebop tradition—the bass drum and toms tuned fairly high and very open, snare drum tight and crisp. Tony's articulation on the drums and cymbals was impeccable, and his consistent sound and touch contributed to his intense time feel.

Tony's ride cymbal had a beautiful combination of great stick definition, more of a "tick" than a "ping," in contrast to a broad, dark cushion of "wash" underneath. His crash was higher-pitched than his ride, responded quickly, and was never used as a second ride. In fact, throughout his career Tony never changed his ride cymbal in the middle of a tune; every soloist received a similar sonic backdrop from which to work. In addition, his hi-hats were on the heavy side and created a dark, full sound.

After Miles

Upon leaving Miles' quintet in 1969 Tony formed his own band, Lifetime, with guitarist John McLaughlin and organist Larry Young. This band was a power trio and perhaps the first true "fusion" band. During this period Tony's playing became even more aggressive and virtuosic. Their recordings, *Emergency* and *Turn It Over*, are very raw-sounding but must be checked out because they contain some of the most ferocious and outrageous drumming ever heard.

In 1975 Tony released a great session with a new band, featuring guitarist Allan Holdsworth, entitled *Believe It*. At this point Tony introduced a completely different drum and cymbal sound, which was geared for the louder, more groove-oriented music of this band. As a leader, Tony continued in this fundamental creative zone, in addition to doing numerous more straight-ahead special projects and record dates, until 1985. He continued to refine this basic drum and cymbal sound for the remainder of his career.

In 1985 Tony formed a new quintet with the same instrumentation as the Miles Davis quintet that he had been a member of in the '60s and returned to recording and touring as a leader in the jazz arena. While Tony continued his mastery of the instrument, his playing was now more "inside"—there were fewer deceptive cadences and the vocabulary was more familiar—almost like he had mastered all the wild stuff that he had been doing earlier. But in mastering that vocabulary, some of the urgent "spark" was taken out of it. The focus of this group, and most of Tony's later energy, seemed to be towards presenting his newly refined, highly developed compositional skills. (This band was captured on the fantastic concert video *Tony Williams New York Live*.)

Tony had, through continuous work and study, become an excellent composer, and he played his own compositions with an awareness of dynamics, pacing, and form that one would expect only from the master musician he truly was. While Tony will be sorely missed, the answers to any questions that one might have about how to play music can be found in each and every one of his recordings.

Thank you, Tony.

Chapter 22

Expanding The Learning Process

A big factor in our growth as musicians is the emulation of those we admire. We do this by imitating or copying the things our idols play. The usual process involves playing along with a recording until we get the "thing" we're attracted to—the sound, the feel, the articulation, the sticking. Most people consider the effort a success once they can play something just like it is on the record. But that's just the *beginning*; you must integrate these new "things" into your vocabulary.

To speed up the integration process, I suggest writing out the ideas you are trying to assimilate. By writing out ideas, you'll not only learn them faster, you will be able to manipulate them and make them "your own." And that's something you can't really do when you play them from memory.

To illustrate how this concept works, I've written out some solos. Below are four bebop-style "fours" (four-measure solos), but this approach works regardless of style. If these "fours" were on a record and you learned them by ear, you could only play them one way—from beginning to end. Having them written down opens up a world of new applications that will help you *own* them.

Obviously the first step is to learn to play each phrase as it is. The stickings will help you get the proper flow. Play the hi-hat on 2 and 4 and play four measures of jazz time between each phrase, swinging the 8th notes. (The tempo can range on these anywhere between quarter note equals 120 and 220 beats per minute.)

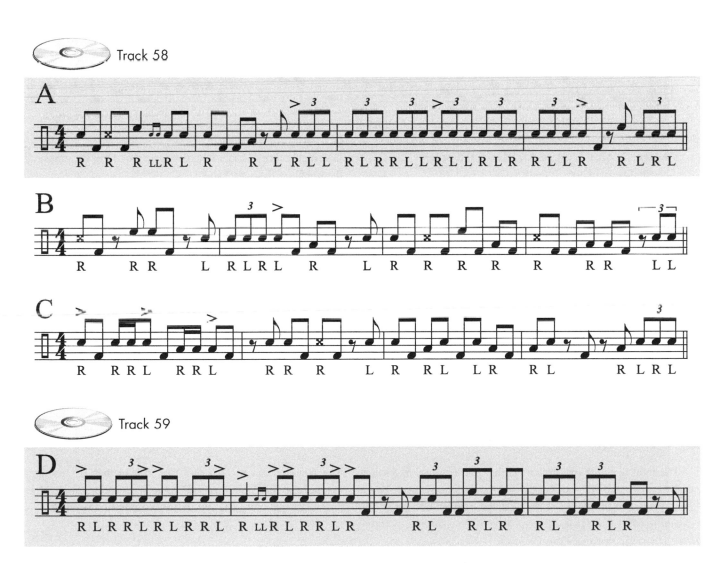

Track 58

Track 59

With some practice you should be able to play the phrases as well as you would if you'd learned them by ear. But let's go a little deeper in the hope that you'll begin to make the phrases your own. Looking at phrase A, play it starting in the second measure. Play A2, 3, 4, 1, in that order.

Track 60

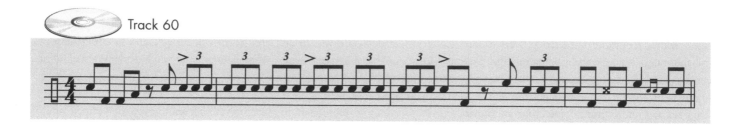

The phrase sounds and feels completely different. Now start on the third measure. Play A3, 4, 1, 2. Start on the fourth measure: A4, 1, 2, 3. Mix it up. Play A1, 3, 4, 2 or 4, 3, 2, 1, and so on. Undoubtedly not every combination will be a "gem," but you will begin to learn and hear this new material more thoroughly and probably come up with some phrases that the originator would never have thought of. Now go through the same process with phrases B, C, and D.

The next step is to combine ideas from the different phrases. For example, play A1, A2, B1, and B2.

Now try A2, A3, C3, C4, or A1, B1, C1, D1, or D3, C2, A4, B2. The possibilities are almost endless.

Let's take it even further. Go back to phrase A and modify it by making the *second* beat of measure one the "1" of the phrase. Play the hi-hat on the new 2 and 4.

Now start the phrase on beat 3…or beat 4…or measure two, beat 2…. Here's phrase D starting on measure two, beat 4.

Track 61

The final result of this process is that you'll sound like someone who has studied—but not *copied*—a particular player. You'll hear your *own* ideas. Consider what the possibilities are if you combine ideas from two different players from different idioms! You would begin to hear and play things that are completely unique, and that's the goal—to come from the tradition of great drummers that preceded you, but still sound like yourself.

The Warm-Up

For years I prepared to play the drums the same way I prepare to exercise: warming up the large muscle groups first by playing large, loud strokes. Using that method, it would take me quite a while to feel loose and ready to play. Recently I've adopted another strategy and experienced faster and more thorough results.

I begin my warm-up very gently, playing easy "drop"-type double strokes—a 4" wrist stroke followed by a bounce—with little regard for speed, sound, or accuracy. (Use the following tempo markings as a guide; a warm-up should be relaxed and smooth, not a chops burnout.)

The first objectives of the warm-up are to remind my hands of the feeling of the rebounding sticks and to get some blood moving in their direction. After a minute or two of playing doubles, my hands will feel the sticks rebounding nicely and the muscles in my forearms will begin to relax and align themselves for drumming. Next I'll move on to a minute or two of drop triple strokes, a wrist stroke followed by two bounces.

Now I'll feel warm enough to play larger, more controlled strokes, and I'll slow the tempo to play a succession of 12" wrist strokes with an overlapping flam.

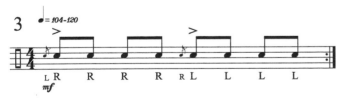

Once the previous move feels good, I'll up the ante and play a combination of singles and paradiddles, like in the following exercise.

My final three warm-up sequences involve flams moving through Swiss Army triplets (example 5), flam accents (6), and flam paradiddles (7). I'll spend a minute or two playing each.

In addition to physically getting ready to play, throughout the warm-up I'm also thinking about what I hope to accomplish once I get to the drums.

Give this ten- to fifteen-minute warm-up a try each day for two weeks and see how it works for you.

Basic Training 1

Why practice technique? The simple answer is to gain more control of our instrument. A more driving reason is our realization that just about every innovator in any field of endeavor, from Michael Jordan to Vinnie Colaiuta, has possessed not only superb technical command, but superior and innovative "moves." Superior and innovative moves are impossible without strong fundamentals.

The technical foundation for great drumming is formed at the snare drum. In my travels I've noticed that many younger players concentrate exclusively on playing the kit, and don't realize that time spent honing the basic motions on the snare drum or a pad will pay big dividends at the drumset. To gain control, relaxation, efficiency, endurance, power, speed, and good time, one must focus on the hands alone and do repetitive drills correctly. Like the TV fitness guru says, "If getting in shape were easy, then everyone would be in shape." If playing the drums were easy….

The exercise below is designed to help you gain more control of your hands. The idea is to repeat each one-measure paradiddle phrase at a relaxed tempo. Play the unaccented notes "low," and use height, not tension, to generate the accents. In order to make the accents "pop" out, you must read ahead and prepare the correct stick heights.

Before you do the paradiddles, try the two warm-up exercises, which go through the cycle of basic stroke moves: the full stroke, which starts and finishes high and is played when you have an accent followed by another accent with the same hand; the down stroke, which starts high and finishes low to create the desired accent and to finish in the most efficient position to play the next soft note; the up stroke, which starts low and finishes high to prepare for the next accent; and the tap, which starts and finishes low and is used for consecutive soft notes by the same hand.

Warm-Up Exercises

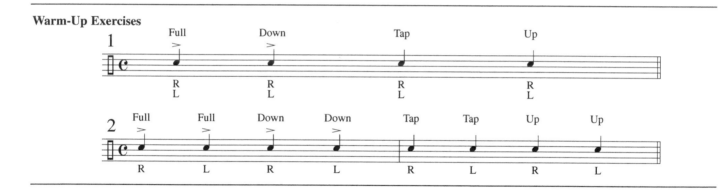

The correct moves for the first paradiddle measure are: The first loud right is a down stroke because the next right is a soft note on beat 2. The next note, a soft left, is an up stroke because the next left is a loud note on beat 3. The next note, a soft right, is a tap. Then the following note is another tap. The note on beat 3 is a loud left down stroke (the left hand should already be in the

"high" position). The next right is soft going to loud—an up stroke. The last two lefts are taps.

Once you're familiar with this approach, practice the exercise by playing each measure four times, then continue down the page. A good starting tempo is quarter note = 50, but the sky's the limit. Just be sure that you maintain control.

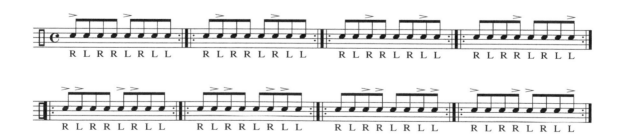

I realize that this kind of choreography is pretty awkward at first, but the resulting gain in control and consistency of sound is worth the effort. In time these motions become second-nature and lead to increased speed, relaxation, and clarity. For more information on the concept, check out Joe Morello's video *The Natural Approach To Technique* and Gary Chaffee's book *Rhythm And Meter, Volume 1*.

Next time we'll dig a little deeper into snare drum fundamentals. Until then, remember that practicing in a slow, relaxed fashion while concentrating on maintaining perfect "form" is much more beneficial in the long run than recklessly muscling it out.

Basic Training 2

In Chapter 24 we discussed fundamental hand-technique issues. To begin this one I'm going to refer to the earlier column and give you several additional ways to practice that page of accented paradiddles. These exercises are control- and speed-builders.

First, every time you have an accented note, convert that accent into an unaccented double stroke.

This…

becomes this:

This…

becomes this:

Second, convert each accent into an unaccented triple stroke.
This…

becomes this:

This…

becomes this:

Third, convert each accent into a flam.
This…

becomes this:

This…

becomes this:

You'll find that the issues related to stick heights are the same as with the original accented paradiddles.

Now let's up the ante and play accented paradiddles in triplets. The triplet rate really creates havoc with making the accented notes flow. As with the new approaches introduced earlier and the original concept (Chapter 24), you must take this material slowly, read ahead, and prepare for each "next move" in order to maintain good form.

If you're really ambitious you can also add double strokes, triple strokes, and flams to the triplet paradiddles.

The Moeller Stroke Revealed
Speed, Endurance...And Drumming's Fountain Of Youth?

Jim Chapin and Joe Morello are among the elder statesman of drumming, yet few players of any age have their technical finesse, power, endurance, or speed. Chapin and Morello have developed and maintained their chops by incorporating the "Fountain Of Youth" of drumming, a technique promoted by legendary performer and educator Sanford A. Moeller.

Jim Chapin was a student of Moeller and is a magnificent teacher and tireless "giver" of Moeller's concepts. If you've ever attended a Percussive Arts Society International Convention or a *Modern Drummer* festival, you've surely seen Jim generously sharing his knowledge with any eager student of drumming. In his video *Speed, Power, Control, Endurance,* Jim clearly demonstrates Moeller's methods, making it a must-have for any drummer seeking to improve his facility.

Another must-have is Joe Morello's video *The Natural Approach To Technique.* When I was in high school I had the good fortune to study with Joe. He taught me that drummers use three groups of muscles: the arm, the wrist, and the fingers. Most playing is done with the wrist, the arm is used for power, while the fingers are used for low-volume speed. Each of the three muscle groups is trained separately, and each hand is trained individually. Eventually everything is integrated. The key was, and still is, to allow the sticks to rebound naturally.

Repetitive actions like a single-stroke roll—played loudly using the arms, at a medium volume using the wrists, or softly using the fin-

gers—naturally cause fatigue. To combat fatigue, drummers "press": We tighten up. This allows us to temporarily persevere by increasing the tension in our grip; we squeeze it out. But in short order, all control breaks down.

Joe developed his "natural" technical concepts by studying with the great old masters of drumming, George L. Stone and Billy Gladstone, and he learned Sanford Moeller's concepts from his first teacher, Joe Sefcik. These masters agreed on the fundamentals of good technique, but zeroed in on different areas: Stone's approach focused mainly on wrist development, Gladstone was more finger-oriented, and Moeller employed a tension-breaking combination stroke. Joe demonstrates the attributes of each of these approaches on his video.

Early in the 1900s, Sanford Moeller realized that one reduces and ultimately eliminates tension by distributing the "load" of repetitive motions among several muscle groups. The Moeller stroke incorporates the arm, wrist, and fingers into one flowing action, and is perfect for playing flowing accents within a single-stroke roll. Once you've mastered the Moeller stroke, you make the motion and the stick almost plays by itself.

To learn this motion, we'll go through the mechanics of the Moeller stroke in slow motion, step-by-step. The more thoroughly you understand these fundamental principles, the easier it will be to make the motion flow at faster tempos. Let's start by putting our sticks down and sitting in front of a large mirror.

Sanford A. Moeller (1879–1961) was born in Albany, New York and lived in the New York City area. Moeller began playing the drums as a teenager (though his first instrument was the piano), studying with August Helmicke of John Phillip Sousa's band.

It's said that Moeller was so curious about the old ways of drumming that, as a young man, he sought out the surviving Civil War drummers and picked their brains about how, why, and what they played. In fact, a publisher's note on page 1 of the *Moeller Book* states that Sanford's teaching style and concepts were based on George B. Bruce's 1862 US Army prescribed drum methods.

Moeller was a renowned maker of Colonial-style rope-tension parade drums. He also coached bugle, fife, and drum corps. Moeller became a sought-after teacher, with Gene Krupa, Jim Chapin, and Frank Ippolito among his many students.

The *Moeller Book* was originally published in 1925 and is still in print. (It's currently being published by Ludwig Music Publishing. 557-67 East 140th Street, Cleveland, Ohio 44110.) I had a copy of it as a kid, and the photographs of his motion intrigued me. But something about them also confused me. I was relieved when Jim Chapin told me that Moeller himself

was unhappy with the way his concepts came across in the photos. Regardless of that, his teaching and those motions became a prime part of two other very popular early drum books—*The Gene Krupa Drum Method* and *The Ludwig Drum Method.*

Sanford, known as "Gus" to his friends, was a cantankerous senior citizen by the time Joe Morello approached him for lessons. Joe told me Moeller took one look at him and, before Joe even played a note,

said, "You don't really want to be a drummer—go home!" Thankfully Joe didn't heed Moeller's advice. And, fortunately for us, through the teaching of Joe and people like Jim Chapin, we can all better understand and utilize the Moeller stroke.

Thanks to Derrick Logozzo and the PAS Archives for biographical information.

John Riley

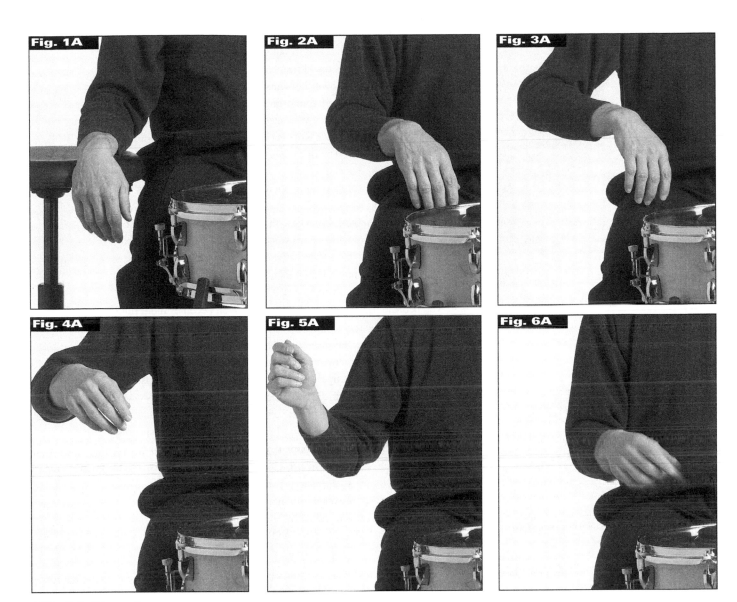

Right Hand

Begin by resting your right forearm on your floor tom or on a table (Figure 1A). Put your wrist joint exactly at the edge, relax, and let your hand hang limply over the side towards the floor. This is a neutral position.

Now, while maintaining your relaxed wrist, slide your arm off the surface. Let your upper arm hang down from the shoulder; don't hold it into or away from your torso (Figure 2A). Allow your forearm to relax in a position parallel to the floor, and let your hand continue to hang towards the floor in a neutral position, with your palm facing down. From this position we can begin to explore the Moeller motion. (Because it accommodates a greater range of motion, the Moeller stroke works much better with a German-type "palms down" grip than it does with the French-type "thumbs up" grip.)

Gently swing your upper arm six inches away from your torso, and allow it to fall naturally back into your body. This action

should cause your limp hand to wiggle a bit (Figure 3A).

Increase the swing to a foot or more, and be sure that your hand remains relaxed.

As your upper arm moves away from the torso, the limp hand stays down (Figure 4A). Now, instead of allowing your arm to simply fall back into your body as before, accelerate towards your body. The instant you change direction and accelerate back towards the torso, the hand is forced to flop up (Figure 5A).

Allow your rapidly moving elbow to bang into your ribs. If you've maintained that limp wrist/hand combination, this acceleration and "pop" into your ribs will snap the hand back to its starting position towards the floor (Figure 6A).

Observe how your hand is "following" the movements of your elbow; try thinking of your arm as a whip and your hand as the tip of the whip. This snapping action is exactly what breaks the tension.

Fig. 7A

Fig. 8A

Now put a stick in your relaxed, "hanging" right hand. Your grip should be as loose and as minimal as possible, but each finger should be in contact with the stick. Your fingers should simply drape around the stick. Now try the motion. Don't worry about the sound, speed, or anything else. Just observe how the movement of your arm controls the action of your hand and the reaction of the stick. Set your metronome at 60 bpm and perform one arm move per beat. If your wrist is supple and "light," the result will most likely be three notes. The first note is loud, and it's the result of your elbow popping into your ribs and snapping your hand back down. Subsequent notes are softer-volume bounces where the hand "rides" the natural motion of the stick.

As you repeat the motion in rhythm, the unaccented notes will occur as a result of your elbow moving away from the torso. (Tip: make your elbow pop into your ribs just before the "click" so that your accented note is synched with the metronome.) Even though your arm has a large range of motion, the stick should play in a small area in the center of the drum.

As you become more comfortable and the motion becomes more fluid, gradually increase the tempo. The three notes will begin to more accurately resemble a triplet. At this early stage of mastery the triplet is perfectly balanced for the Moeller motion. When used for groups of two notes, the arm pumps too fast. When trying to make four notes between whips, your stick runs out of momentum. Figure 7A shows the motion at a moderate speed and catches the action just as the elbow is about to change direction and accelerate back towards the torso. (In the photo, the motion "shadowing" shows the "future"—the direction my hand will be going.)

Figure 8A catches the motion a fraction of a second later, just as the elbow pops into the torso and snaps the wrist back towards the drum. (The "shadowing" shows where the hand is going.)

Now that you have an idea about the motion, let's check it in the mirror one more time. Put your stick down and make the motion. Though your elbow is moving quite a distance from side-to-side, your hand should have less side-to-side movement.

When you get above 120 bpm, the motion shrinks and has much less of an elbow swing. (This makes it difficult to capture on film.) The wrist snap, which is crucial to breaking the tension of repeated actions, is accomplished in a slightly different, more compact fashion: With the wrist limp, raise the forearm four inches while allowing your hand to hang down like before. Now snap your forearm down. Use a force similar to when you snapped your elbow into your torso, so that your wrist flops up and is whipped back down. Try visualizing a cobra recoiling and then striking a target on the ground. Your forearm is the body of the snake, and your hand is the snake's head. This should produce a faster version of the original motion. If you have further questions about this, refer to the videos mentioned above.

If you play matched grip, use your right hand and the directions above as a guide for the left hand. Everything works the same way. If you play traditional grip, the fundamentals for the left hand are exactly the same, but the starting position is a little different.

Fig. 1B

Fig. 2B

Fig. 3B

Fig. 4B

Fig. 5B

Fig. 6B

Left Hand

Rest your left hand as shown in figure 1B above, and let your wrist hang.

Now move your left forearm off the surface and rest it in a position with your wrist, hand, and fingers relaxed (Figure 2B). Your forearm should be parallel to the floor. Rotate your forearm counter-clockwise so that the palm of your hand is perpendicular to the floor. The back of your hand should be in line with, and an extension of, your forearm. This is the left-hand traditional-grip starting position.

Gently swing your upper arm about six inches away from your torso, and allow it to fall naturally back into your body (Figure 3B). This action should cause your limp hand to wiggle. Increase the swing to a foot or more, and notice that your left hand remains relaxed (Figure 4B).

Now, instead of allowing your arm to simply fall back into your body, accelerate. The instant you change direction and accelerate back towards your torso, the left hand is forced to flop up (Figure 5B).

Allow your rapidly moving elbow to bang into your ribs. If you've maintained that limp wrist/hand combination, this acceleration and "pop" into your ribs will snap the hand back to its starting position (Figure 6B).

Fig. 7B

Fig. 8B

Again, observe how your hand is "following" the movements of your elbow; think of your left arm as a whip and your hand as the tip of the whip. Check the flow of the motion in a mirror.

Now put the stick in your relaxed, traditional-grip left hand. Let the stick "sit" in the fleshy web between your thumb and first finger. Bring the index finger over the stick. Don't clamp your thumb down on the stick. Allow your middle finger to "ride" alongside the stick, while gently curling your fourth finger and pinky under the stick towards the palm. Repeat the process as described above to get the feel of how the stick responds to the movements of the arm.

Figure 7B catches the left-hand motion at a moderate tempo, just as the elbow is about to change direction and accelerate

towards the torso. (The motion "shadowing" shows where my hand is headed.)

Figure 8B is a fraction of a second later, just as the elbow pops into the torso and snaps the wrist back towards the drum. (Here the shadowing shows where my hand has been.)

At faster tempos the left hand motion shrinks too. It becomes a side-to-side forearm flick that snaps the wrist and breaks the tension. Be sure to maintain a loose wrist throughout the entire motion cycle.

To help you develop this concept, practice the following exercises to reinforce and master the motion. Remember, the whipping motion generates the accented notes.

Eventually you'll be able to employ a more random and less-accented "mini" whipping motion to produce "wave"-like single-stroke rolls at fast tempos. In time, it's possible to work this "stress free" motion to speeds in excess of triplets at 200 bpm.

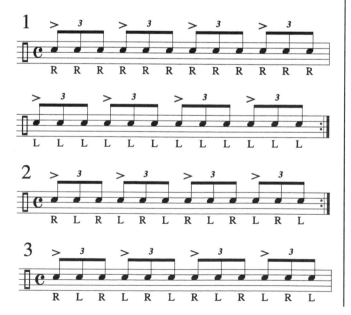

Danny Gottlieb, JoJo Mayer, Ed Soph, Dom Famularo, Vinnie Colaiuta, and many others can all be seen capitalizing on the mechanical advantages of the Moeller motion. Dom's book *It's Your Move* includes very good information on the stroke.

Be patient and relaxed as you go about perfecting the Moeller motion. Use this text and photos as your guide. Develop the whip slowly in front of a mirror, and refer to the videos mentioned above. But start working on it today!

More Moeller

n this Chapter we'll explore some of the drumset applications of the Moeller stroke. You may want to refer back to Chapter 26 before working on the examples here.

Although the stroke was originally used while standing and playing on a parade drum, the motion is perfectly suited for today's drumset player. I use the motion to help me play a wide array of brisk repeated notes in either hand or both hands together.

The Moeller stroke works perfectly when playing a fast bossa nova. Use the whipping action to execute accents on the cymbal in unison with the cross-stick on the snare drum.

Track 62

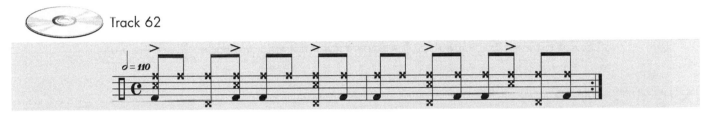

When playing up-tempo jazz, vary the cymbal pattern by interspersing groups of repeated notes that are accomplished incorporating Moeller strokes.

Moeller also works great for adding variety to comping. At medium tempos, play triplets on the snare drum. The whipping action can be used to create accents on downbeats or upbeats.

Track 63

Playing triplets phrased in groups of four notes creates a hip hemiola.

Contrapuntal solo material can be developed by playing a Moeller ostinato in one hand while playing syncopated phrases with the other hand.

Track 64

Chapter 26 contains exercises for developing the motion. Those same phrases can be played on the drumset. Try putting some of the accented notes on the toms.

Experiment with Moeller. Refine the motion through repetition on the practice pad, and then have fun with it on the drumset.

The Pyramid
Challenging Your Hands, Mind, And Ears

New ideas often challenge us on different levels—the technical, conceptual, and sonic. For some years I've been exploring the concepts of implied time and metric modulation. The phrases that follow have grown out of that exploration and will challenge your hands, mind, and ears. They employ sticking patterns of five, six, and seven notes, organized to imply the jazz ride cymbal pattern played at various rates of speed.

Our foundation rhythm is the six-note triplet pattern played RLLRLR. Example 1 shows this sticking at four different rates of speed. Then it sequences the patterns to create a four-measure phrase (example 1a). This gives the impression of speeding up and slowing down. Play each pattern on a pad or snare drum. Once it begins to flow, play it on two different sound sources.

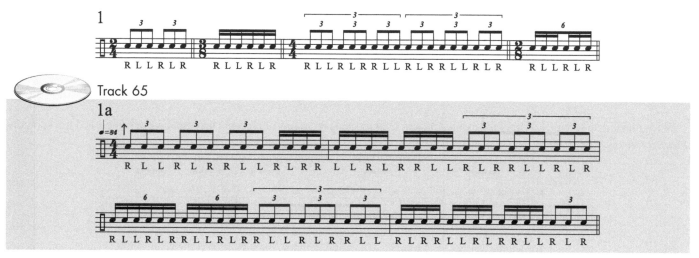

Track 65

Examples 2 and 3 go through the same kind of process with five- and seven-note sticking patterns.

Track 66

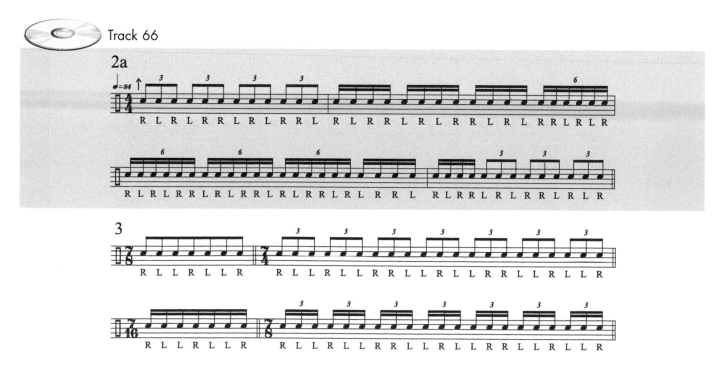

3a

R L L R L L R R L L R L   L R R L L R L L R R L L R L L

R R L L R L L R R L L R L L R R L L R L L R   R L L R L L R R L L R L L R

Practice example 4 to get comfortable shifting between the five-, six-, and seven-note sticking patterns at the 16th-note rate. I've added accents to suggest the "2 and 4" of the ride pattern. Once it flows, try it on two different sound sources.

4

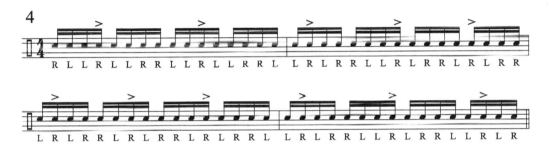

R L L R L L R R L L R L L R R L   L R L R R L L R L R R L R L R R

L R L R R L R L R R L R L R R L   L R L R R L L R L R R L L R L R

The final example is a pyramid where, over the course of twelve measures, we link the various sticking patterns together to create the illusion of a very gradual acceleration until, in the seventh bar, the original tempo is doubled. Then a very gradual deceleration begins that leads back to the original time feel. While each separate time-shifting phrase might already be familiar, the seamless sequencing of them and finding the exact points to shift from one to another is crucial.

I've written the pyramid out with the hands split between the ride cymbal and snare drum, but first play through it on one surface. Set your metronome to quarter note = 60, and tap your foot with the click.

5

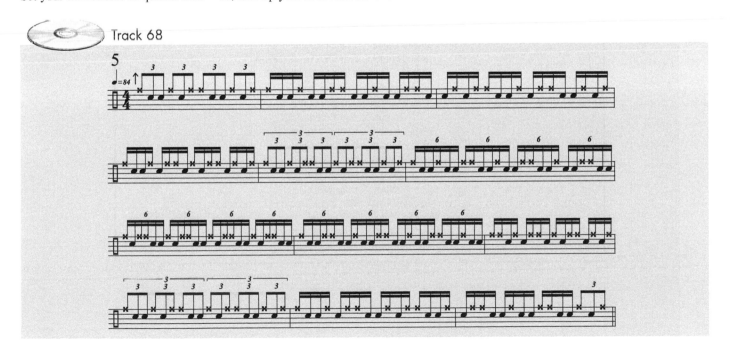

Now go back and play the pyramid as written on your ride cymbal and snare drum. Use a metronome, and play quarter notes along with it on your bass drum, and 2 and 4 on the hi-hat, to help stabilize your pulse. Once you're comfortable with that, play the snare drum part on your leg so that you really hear the cymbal beat accelerating and decelerating.

Finally, play the "bongo beat" with your left hand. Here's how it fits with each of the sticking patterns.

Best of luck with this material, and feel free to use these concepts to explore fresh fill and solo ideas as well.

Essential Listening

Here's a list of the recordings mentioned in this text.
Please refer to these CDs to help you get deeper into the sound and feeling of the music.

Artist	Album
Michael Brecker	Time Is Of The Essence
Clifford Brown And Max Roach	Clifford Brown And Max Roach
Clifford Brown And Max Roach	Incorporated
Clifford Brown And Max Roach	Live At Basin Street
Dave Brubeck	Time Out
Ornette Coleman	The Shape Of Jazz To Come
John Coltrane	Crescent
John Coltrane	Plays The Blues
Miles Davis	Four And More
Miles Davis	Nefertiti
Miles Davis	Workin'
Dexter Gordon	Go
Herbie Hancock	Takin' Off
Eddie Harris	The In Sound
Roy Haynes	Out Of The Afternoon
Hank Jones	The Oracle
Joe Lovano	Trio Fascination
Lee Morgan	The Sidewinder
Tito Puente	Top Percussion
Max Roach	Drums Unlimited
Max Roach	Conversation
Sonny Rollins	Newk's Time
Wayne Shorter	Night Dreamer
Michael Spiro	Bata Ketu
McCoy Tyner	The Real McCoy
Tony Williams	Believe It!
Tony Williams	Emergency
Tony Williams	Turn It Over